DESIGNING MESSAGES FOR
DEVELOPMENT COMMUNICATION

DESIGNING MESSAGES FOR DEVELOPMENT COMMUNICATION

An Audience Participation-Based Approach

BELLA MODY

Illustrations by Mary Rolston Singh

SAGE Publications
New Delhi/Newbury Park/London

For Rosette Mody

Copyright © Bella Mody, 1991

First published in 1991 by

Sage Publications India Pvt Ltd
M-32 Greater Kailash Market I
New Delhi 110 048

Sage Publications Inc
2455 Teller Road
Newbury Park, California 91320

Sage Publications Ltd
6 Bonhill Street
London EC2A 4PU

Published by Tejeshwar Singh for Sage Publications India Pvt Ltd, photo-typeset by Jayigee Enterprises, and printed at Chaman Offset Printers.

Library of Congress Cataloging-in-Publication Data

Mody, Bella,
    Designing messages for development communication: an audience participation-based approach/Bella Mody: illustrations by Mary Rolston Singh
    p. cm. — (Communication and human values)
    Includes bibliographical references and index.
    1. Mass media—Developing countries. 2. Mass media—Audiences.
I. Title. II. Series: Communication and human values (Newbury Park, Calif.)
    P92.2.M64 302.23 09172 4—dc 20 1991 91–28765

ISBN 0–8039–9105–3 (US-hbk) 81–7036–250–4 (India-hbk)
       0–8039–9106–1 (US-pbk) 81–7036–251–2 (India-pbk)

'...discouraged citizens of free countries tell themselves that they have no voice in the nation's affairs, that their actions are useless, that their voice is not heard, and that the elections are fixed. Such people claim that *the press and radio are in the hands of a few*, that they cannot prevent war, or demand peace, or even obtain from their elected representatives that for which they were sent to parliament. However, they recognise that they possess the right to do so...after all, they are responsible for their own freedom.'

From Albert Memmi, *The Colonizer and the Colonized*. Boston, Massachusetts: Beacon Press, 1967, pp. 91–92 (emphasis added).

CONTENTS

PREFACE

This *audience participation-based approach* to the design of media messages is an outgrowth of my experience with communication projects in India, Nepal, Thailand, Malaysia, Jamaica, Barbados, Costa Rica, Liberia, Kenya, Zimbabwe,

Tanzania, and Ghana. *Designing Messages for Development Communication* focuses on the problems of designing audience-responsive messages in the Third World. As such, it reviews the literature on communication effects, in the context of a subset of the literature on communication for development.

Many multilateral and bilateral foreign aid agencies (e.g., UNESCO, UNICEF, the US Agency for International Development) invested in mass media projects supportive of agriculture, health, family planning, and formal education during the first and second United Nations Development Decades (1960–1980). Each project prepared very useful 'how-to' manuals, which were mimeographed or printed in limited numbers. The projects' manuals disappeared when foreign funding and local government support ended. New projects commissioned new manuals, all saying much the same thing, except that they were designed for different sectors (e.g., health versus agriculture) or for different media (e.g., radio versus television).

This is a **'do-it-yourself' text on audience participation-based message design in Third World settings**. It focuses on national transformation. As such, its applicability cuts across all public service areas and national development sectors (agriculture, health, nutrition, family planning, formal and nonformal education). The ideal audience participation-based message design procedure will be the same, irrespective of the goal, the capital-intensity of the medium (posters versus magazines, television versus audio cassettes), or the size of the audience. Whenever the target audience is separated from the message design team, there is one common sense starting place: the audience. **Begin with the audience. Listen. Observe**. This book focuses on the audience research process; it is not designed to teach production skills.

I started my career as a designer of communication messages in the late 1960s, in what was then a United States advertising agency in Calcutta, India. I was trained to write advertising copy on the job. For almost two years, I wrote text for ads promoting products ranging from trucks, to steel, to lavender soap. The ad agency's air-conditioned offices overlooked one of Calcutta's many slums. Its ads exhorted those with purchasing power to buy their way to happiness while more than half of Calcutta went to bed hungry every night. A Catholic Jesuit priest from New Jersey who founded the Communication Institute at St. Xavier's College suggested that

I might find it more congenial to work on public service applications of mass media. The Rev. 'Packy' McFarland saw a need for India to use the mass media to support national development. He proposed that I go to a university in the United States to learn how this can be done. The irony in my going to the center of the world's business system to learn communication skills appropriate for non-profit applications in a Third World country escaped my notice, as a 22-year-old. Packy has given up on centrally controlled mass media and now works with small group media in Nigeria.

At the University of Pennsylvania in the late 1960s, I learned that the media had actually been less powerful than expected. The mass media had provided information, but families, friends, and neighbors ultimately influenced the decisions people made and the actions they took. I also read the optimistic writings of Daniel Lerner, Wilbur Schramm, and Everett M. Rogers, who claimed that the mass media could transform the Third World. Who was right, I wondered. My challenge was to make sense of these co-existing bodies of literature, one cautious, the other wildly enthusiastic.

My work with a Philadelphia advertising agency in the summer of 1970 taught me that conducting consumer research before developing ads helped reduce the odds against communicating effectively through the mass media. Also, the success of the educational television show, *Sesame Street*, was instructive. The *Sesame Street* audience acquired a great deal of learning through exposure to this wonderful television show. Unfortunately, this success failed to bridge the historical gap between the educational achievements of White preschool children and those belonging to politically and economically disadvantaged races, despite intensive preproduction audience research. I learned that message designers must be realistic in setting goals. The media cannot substitute for political and economic resource reallocations.

Returning to India, I worked for six years on the design and evaluation of television programs that supported agriculture extension, health education, nutrition, family planning, and formal education. These programs were delivered to remote villages by a communication satellite. With my colleagues on the Satellite Instructional Television staff in the Indian Space Research Organization, I wondered: what good can words and images on a television screen do for that half of the country's population that lives in poverty, given that their poverty is caused by enormous differences in the distribution of agricultural land? Even most of the poor consider their plight to be inevitable. How can television programs produced by a well-intentioned government agency counteract religious, cultural, and political forces that perpetuate acceptance of such economic inequality and social injustice?

My Indian colleagues and I mixed political economy from Marx and Gramsci with Paulo Freire's consciousness-raising approach to education. To that, we added what we knew about advertising campaign design to develop a systematic audience research-based approach to message design. These years of experience in the field provided the basis for the courses I taught in Communication and Development and in Audience Research for Message Design at Stanford University from 1978–1983, at San Francisco State University in 1984, and currently teach at Michigan State University.

I applied the audience research-based approach that we developed in the Indian Space Research Organization to the design of a community radio station in central Jamaica from 1979 to 1982. This project was funded by the governments of Jamaica and the United States. I have also been able to share the common sense fundamentals of the audience research-based approach with radio producers in Zimbabwe (financed by UNESCO), with Caribbean Women's Project staff in Barbados (funded by the German Friedrich-Ebert Foundation), and with AIDS prevention health communicators in Tanzania, Ghana, and India (for the World Health Organization).

This handbook shows media producers in public service agencies how to give *systematic attention* to the audience, so that decisions regarding sound, motion, and lighting reflect the preferences and customs of their audiences. It focuses on *audience involvement* in the production of mass media messages. I wrote *Designing Messages for Development Communication* with an audience-research emphasis for two kinds of readers:

1. Media users and media producers in governmental and nongovernmental organizations who produce messages to support national development programs, whether they work in big centralized agencies or in decentralized grassroots organizations.

2. Students and professors of development communication who want to learn about audience participation in message design.

The highlighted boxes are illustrative cases of practical significance. Students and their professors will want to read the whole book for details of theory and procedure.

After reading this book, the media writer, graphic artist, videographer, filmmaker, development planner, and communication planner will

FIRST listen to the audience *before beginning message design* to determine which information the audience needs, and in what form (e.g., rational, emotional, folkloric, modern, musical or dramatic) they can process it most effectively, and

THEN pretest 'draft' messages on the audience, *midproduction*, before the messages are produced in final form for distribution via the mass media.

My father points out that common sense tells him the things that we communication researchers take pages to obfuscate in 'scholarly' books and journals. My justification for writing a book expounding self-evident common sense is that common sense is so rarely applied. I hope that the appearance of this common sense approach between Sage covers will clothe it in the legitimacy it needs to be deemed worthy of widespread application in Third World settings. In this form, it may outlive the good fugitive manuals produced in the Third World.[1]

The random numbers table in Chapter 6 is reprinted from David B. Owen, *Handbook for Statistical Tables*, 1962, with permission from Addison Wesley Publishing Company. The case study of Jamaican radio in Chapter 4 is adapted from my article entitled, 'The Receiver as Sender: Formative Evaluation in Jamaican Radio', in *Gazette*, vol. 38, 1986, with the permission of its publisher.

WACC has contributed towards the editing, graphics, and production costs of this book in order that the sales price be within the reach of Third World students. My Michigan State University colleague Charles Atkin very generously responded to my erratic requests for updates on the US communication effects literature and commented on an earlier draft of this manuscript, as did Everett M. Rogers. Rogers hired me to teach at Stanford University in 1978. Although both of us left Stanford in the early 1980s, and our intellectual and political perspectives often differ, Rogers has continued to be a supportive colleague. I am grateful to the anonymous Sage reviewer for very constructive suggestions. Poonam Sreen-Smith assisted in the organization of literature that is reviewed in this book. This text has been keyed into the computer by several Michigan State University support staff in Urban Affairs Programs. Hence, the consistent use of US English spelling even though my first language is Indian English. My secretary, Fran Fowler, struggled with good humor through several versions, while handling a full secretarial load. Shirley Hoksbergen incorporated the suggestions of Michael Traber and Shelton Gunaratne on a penultimate draft. Lynn Anderson edited parts of this version. All remaining errors in form and substance are due to my intransigence, oversight, and indigestion.

February 1991   *Bella Mody*

Notes

1. A good example is Dr. Farag Elkamel's *Developing Communication Strategies and Programs: A Systematic Approach*, produced by UNICEF's Mena Regional Office in 1986.

DEVELOPMENT COMMUNICATION 1

Development means development of the bottom 50 percent of a country.
—*Mohammed Yunus, Founder of the Grameen Bank, Bangladesh.*

The shared aspiration of three and a half billion people (two-thirds of the world's population) who live in Asia, Africa, Latin America, the Middle East, and the Caribbean is to escape from poverty to a better life. Different peoples have different visions of what human betterment and national development is, and how to work towards it. How should interested graphic artists and electronic media producers help transform the lives of the majority of humanity (the two-thirds in the world) who live on the margins of the industrialized North? How does mass media performance in the South (also referred to as developing countries or the Third World) today compare with idealistic perceptions of its national development potential in the early 1960s? This chapter briefly outlines arguments in the literature on national development and then communication to help media producers understand the implications of choosing particular development frameworks and specific communication strategies within them.[1]

WHAT KIND OF DEVELOPMENT?

Most countries of the South which won national independence after World War II wanted to become 'modern' like Western Europe and North America. Both the United States and USSR power blocs (given the Cold War rivalry) recommended *economic planning* as a means to this end, and offered technical assistance to build the one-time colonies of Asia, the Caribbean, and Africa, in keeping with their own market needs and foreign policy objectives. The North and the South assumed that planning for technologically-based growth would make it possible for the South to have an industrial revolution of sorts without repeating European history, that is, without suffering their own equivalents of the Crusades, mercantile explorations, colonial plunder, political revolutions, economic exploitation, and cultural degradation that the North went through. Economic growth and modernization planners in the North and South did not foresee the enormous complexity of the events, and their inability to control them.

Factors that were neglected in the planning process were: (*a*) the impact of external forces (dominant nations, banks, corporations) and (*b*) the obstacles that domestic economic, political, and cultural structures would present.

External Forces

The economic development of Western Europe was not strictly an internal affair. Western European colonizers benefitted from their economic exploitation of the resources of the South. The economic development of industrialized Europe distorted and destroyed the economic and technical development and the cultural coherence of countries they ruled. In the 1960s, the rate of growth in the South averaged 6 percent per year. The external environment deteriorated significantly in the 1970s, characterized by international monetary instability and the rise in oil prices in 1973. External forces continued to be uncongenial to the development of the South in the 1980s: growth stopped or reversed in most of Africa and Latin America due to the oil shocks of the 1970s. Official development assistance stagnated. The oil price-related recession in the North led to increased interest rates on the loans they had advanced to the South, and reductions in orders for commodities that the South exported. It was hard for countries of the South to continue their interest payments. As a result, commercial banks were reluctant to continue lending to the South. The South had no choice but to turn to the International Monetary Fund (IMF). In return for renegotiating their outstanding debts, the IMF required 'restructuring' of the debtor countries' economies: increase exports, let market forces prevail, cut back on government spending on health, education, and subsidies, they were instructed. By the mid-1980s, instead of technologically advanced nations transferring resources to facilitate the development of technologically less advanced nations, there was a net negative flow from the South to the North. The living standards of the poor declined sharply in all countries with debt problems. By the end of the 1980s, the prices of commodities that the South exported reached their lowest level in sixty years. Export earnings fell as interest rates increased. Thus, foreign debts required nearly $ 200 billion a year in debt servicing alone.[2,3] The effects of the 1991 Gulf War can only worsen a bad situation for the South, through increased oil prices and reduced overseas employment possibilities for their labor.

Two approaches which focus on external forces as major determinants of national development in the South are dependency analysis and world system analysis. Latin American researchers[4] were among the first to point out that in spite of almost a hundred years of supposed independence, they continued to be dependent on the markets, capital, and technology of Western Europe, North America, and more recently, Japan. In spite of its multiple strands, in general, dependency analysts showed how forces external to a nation influence the state, economic classes, and consequently its national development and development communication activities. These external forces include the foreign policies of leading industrial nations (such as the United States, Germany, and Japan), transnational profit-making firms (such as Warner, Reuters, Philips, Siemens, Sony, and IBM headquartered in the North), international lenders (like Citibank and Chase Manhattan), intergovernmental agencies (such as the International Monetary Fund, the World Bank, the General Agreement on Tariffs and Trade, UNESCO, UNICEF, and the ITU), and bilateral aid agencies (such as USAID, SIDA, CIDA, and the Japanese International Corporation Agency JICA). World system analysts[5,6] argue that any long-term, large-scale social change (such as Third World development) can be understood only in the context of the world capitalist system. World system analysis differs from dependency in that the former focuses on the dynamics of the whole system linked together as an interstate system while the latter focuses on relationships between the Third World part of the system (the periphery) and the core (the First World).

Internal Forces

Economic development plans were aborted by the social system internal to Third World Countries, e.g., power blocs of large landowners (which influence who gets elected) resisted laws to change inequitable distribution of agricultural land. Thus, continuing internal inequality in wealth and economic resources (a few own the land and factories, the majority are labor), social status (in terms of religion, caste, race, tribe, clan), and political power are causes of continuing fatalism, apathy, and low aspirations among the *have-nots* in countries of the South. In the 1970s, researchers found that the gross national product had increased, but that its major beneficiaries were the middle and higher income groups. The already powerful and privileged benefitted from new opportunities created by economic development plans, while the position of the handicapped majority remained the same or became worse.[7] In India, local castes with some economic power and mobility made use of improvements in printing, the postal system, and roads to strengthen and expand their organization on a regional basis. Low castes with no purchasing power to make use of these new technologies could not organize to expand in similar fashion.[8] Thus, to those that have, more was given.

Development planners learned that the choice of development strategy must recognize differences in *access to opportunities for improvement* within a nation, and between nations. Development would have to include mobilization and reorganization of the marginalized majority (within the world community, and individuals within a nation) to counteract the continued monopolization of all opportunities for growth by a strong minority.

The United Nations Development Program's 1990 analysis[9] of the last three decades of development focuses on a comprehensive view of *human* development. Their findings indicate that the link between economic growth and human development is not automatic. While North-South income gaps have widened, fairly respectable levels of human development have been reached at fairly modest levels of income. Until the uneven distribution of income in most countries of the South is changed, food and health subsidies that will transfer income and other opportunities to the poor are recommended. National development must focus on mobilizing human potential through (*a*) access to *material* resources like good health, education, housing, and food, and (*b*) creation of a *culture* and environment that guarantees freedom, human rights, and personal self-respect. A participatory approach is essential. The United Nations Economic Commission for Africa and a number of citizen groups which met in Arusha in February 1989 explicitly identified lack of popular participation as the primary cause of Africa's crisis. Overcentralization of power in the state in Africa had constrained the motivation of its people and underutilized their creativity. The failure of governmental organizations to involve the people and meet their needs has led to the steady growth of nongovernmental grass roots organizations. The South Commission points to the central role of such grass roots groups in people-centered development.

A national, people-centered development plan of action must attack the *causes* of a nation's domination and dependency in the world system, and the internal cultural, economic, and political mechanisms that have been historically and contemporaneously used to marginalize its majority. This implies transformation of the multiple oppressions of gender, class, race, nation, and private corporation, *through participatory democratic decision making*. Women's voices must enter into essential national discussion on how to divert resources from foreign and domestic wars to social welfare, how to eradicate poverty, how to provide opportunities for full development of human potential, how to develop relationships characterized by women's values of nurturance, and how both men and women can share child care.[10] Imitation of Western mass consumption is not an end in itself or an economically viable option on a global scale since the world's resources cannot sustain such development. Continued monopolization of the benefits of growth by a small proportion (of nations or individuals) is not a politically viable option in the long run. The Dag Hammerskjold Foundation and its *Development Dialogue* journal have pioneered such an alternative conceptualization which they call *Another Development*. Presented under the label of a *multiplicity paradigm* by Jan Servaes,[11] this development alternative is based on needs, local self-reliance, ecology, and structural transformation to enable self-management. The central idea of the multiplicity framework is that there is no universal development model; it is a process that will differ from society to society. Development is a relative term.

The road to development advocated in this book is not new. It is basically *grass roots participation* in decisions on the design and implementation of the particular kind of national transformation desired. The end is to give people's lives back to them—free from domination by colonial powers, an authoritarian state, transnational corporations, and structures of inequality such as caste and class. The mass media are useful if they promote mass participation as a means and as an end. The South cannot be blindly imitative since the complexity, scale, and intensity of social, economic, and political mobilization it needs for transformation are quite distinct from anything the North ever needed or experienced. The means of mass participation and mobilization for national transformation cannot be identical in different countries of the South either, because of their distinct histories, geography, economics, and culture. The ends *and* the means are processual and identical: mass participation in decision making *for* mass participation in decision making. Although each nation at different points in time will choose different objective indicators to work towards, it would be naive to believe that the process of national transformation will be short-term or free of conflict, given the contradictory ambitions of different classes within a society.

Who will take the initiative to do this? National development planning and implementation is initiated by the state in most Third World countries. Most Third World states have a dominant single party system, a strong military, and an entrenched civil service administration. In many cases, the state represents the dominant ethnic group, economic class, or political party. In some cases, the state merely reflects tensions and tussles among cultural, economic, and political groups within its boundaries. Sometimes, it tries to be impartial, while at other times, it is allied with a particular group. Sometimes, it is aggressive, and at other times, it allows itself to be attacked, depending on where its interests in ensuring its own economic consolidation and political expansion lie. The ruling classes use the state's repressive apparatus (e.g., military, police, judicial and penal system) and the state's ideological apparatus (e.g., schools, political parties, trade unions, sports activities, and the mass media) to maintain their dominance and win the cooperation of the masses to fulfill their own private agendas.[12] Can the typical Third World state that gives low importance to basic structural change and popular participation, irrespective of whether or not it is elected, be capable of *national* development in favor of the interests of its majority, rather than in the interests of a dominant class, gender, region, or tribe? This is where nongovernmental agencies come in to promote *solidarity networks of countervailing organizations of marginalized majorities* to counteract these dominant groups.

WHY MEDIA FOR DEVELOPMENT SUPPORT?

The first major research on the role of the mass media in national development in a Third World society was conducted by political scientist Daniel Lerner. *The Passing of Traditional Society* published in 1958[13] presents Lerner's version of how the West modernized: increased urbanization led to increased literacy and mass media exposure which led to higher incomes and voting. Lerner speculated that the mechanism that would cause the mass media to promote income growth and political participation was empathy, being able to imagine oneself in another's situation. Was the reality of national development in the Third World that simple?

Subsequent events did not support Lerner's expectations but his work was followed by a flurry of activity. A UNESCO study[14] found that indicators of national development such as per capita income, literacy, urbanization, and industrialization were correlated with indicators of a well-developed media infrastructure (e.g., newsprint consumption per person, daily newspaper circulation per 100 persons, cinema seats per 100 persons and number of radio sets per 100 persons). The development of the mass media was clearly related to other developments in the country. The question, of course, was: which causes what? Do increases in channel availability lead to increases in income, literacy, urbanization, and industrialization, or is it the other way around? Does a third set of factors (e.g., political power) cause both development of the media infrastructure and the development of other dimensions of the nation? Predominantly journalists, the communication professionals staff in UNESCO at the time did not ponder overtly over these questions of directionality in Lerner's statistical correlations. The relationship was positive enough for them to set the minimum media standards that all countries should strive towards. This was followed by MIT political scientist Lucian Pye's collection[15] of readings on how communication channels would promote political development in the Third World along Western lines, and David McClelland's[16] enthusiasm for injecting imagery into mass media channels that would promote achievement motivation in less developed countries.

US communication researcher and teacher Wilbur Schramm was invited by a then primarily US-influenced UNESCO to examine the role of the mass media in promoting social and economic progress. *Mass Media and National Development*, published in 1964,[17] was the result. Strongly infected by Lerner's excitement, Schramm's very readable book laid out a rather optimistic scenario. The media had a lot of potential and promise. They *could* carry mass mobilization messages for national transformation, Schramm felt. But, given the social system, would they? And, did they?

During the United Nations Decade for Development in the 1960s, sociologists in the United States studying how agricultural innovations spread in the US Midwest wondered whether their 'diffusion model' could be of help in the Third World.[18] Diffusion researchers conceived of *Social Change* in terms of *Invention + Diffusion*. They wanted to promote social change in the Third World by promoting the adoption of inventions of the West in technologically less advanced countries. They found that the innovators and early adopters of innovations in a society were in a minority, and were invariably higher in education and socioeconomic status. How to take the majority (lower in education and socioeconomic status) from awareness to interest to trial of innovations at an accelerated pace? Diffusion researchers found the mass media to be useful in generating awareness and interest about an innovation; face-to-face communication was essential at decision making. Thus, the mass media found prominence among another body of social scientists as a means to expeditiously 'diffuse' modern scientific ways of knowing, feeling, and doing among the peasants of Asia, Africa, Latin America, and the Caribbean.

Like the economists[19] on whose foundation they modeled their proposal, proponents of a role for communication media in national development neglected to design their prescriptions to fight resistance from prevailing internal and external power structures.[20] United States and United States-trained political scientists, sociologists, and psychologists (as we will see in the next sections) planned for the diffusion of a 'modern' culture—Western ideas, values, attitudes, and know-how. They did not understand traditional structures of domination, and how large landlords, caste hierarchies, and racial perceptions would continue to perpetuate a subculture characterized by low motivation for achievement and a high need for affiliation.[21] The haves were a major cause of the problem, but change programs focused on the have-nots. Television programs were designed for agricultural workers and owners of marginal landholdings with limited access to seeds, credit, irrigation, and pesticides found themselves at the receiving end of tips from agricultural television programs they could not use.

Media use for education and national development in the Third World was promoted by UNESCO and USAID initiatives in the 1960s. Philanthropic foundations (e.g., Ford) played a small role at the time. Sales promotion efforts by equipment manufacturers (e.g., Philips) were insignificant in the 1960s compared to subsequent Japanese efforts. USAID has been the most active source of government-to-government aid for media applications for national development. UNESCO and USAID collaborated on a research project directed by Wilbur Schramm that resulted in a four-volume series of books for educational planners in 1967. The case studies they produced ranged from applications of radio in India, Thailand, Japan, Togo, Niger, Australia, New Zealand, and the Honduras, to television in American Samoa, the United States, Niger, Colombia, Peru, the Ivory Coast, Italy, and Nigeria.[22, 23] With USAID's mid-1970 shift to rural development of the poorest nations came an emphasis on making the best use of low-cost, broad-coverage media, namely radio. The focus of attention was not which media, but how to incorporate audience research into message design to enhance communication effectiveness and educational impact through a locally available low-cost medium accessible to the majority. In 1977, the World Bank produced two volumes of case studies highlighting the successful uses of radio in Nicaragua, Mexico, Indonesia, Kenya, the Dominican Republic, Honduras, Tanzania, Senegal, Canada, and Alaska.[24] While development communication researchers were writing about the appropriateness of *radio* in Third World conditions for upgrading educational quality, expanding access, and keeping costs down,[25] politicians, upper and middle classes, traders, and advertisers in the South were pushing for the introduction of *television*. Their reasons were entertainment (for the upper and middle classes), profits (for advertisers and other business), and a new medium of propaganda (for the ruling party). The guise was television's visual superiority as a teaching medium for nations with low literacy levels. The scientific findings on lack of significant differences in instructional effectiveness between media were ignored: research on *instructional effectiveness* overwhelmingly concludes that 'there are no significant differences' *between* media.[26] Audiences learn as well from print materials, slides, movies, computers, radio, video, and television. When nations adopt one medium over another, the real reasons are economic, political, and technological, not educational.

Given scarce resources, how crucial is mass media infrastructure for the development process? Printed material and electronic gadgets do not put food in the mouths of the hungry, clothe the naked, and heal the sick. Given the conceptualization (belated, but central) that mass participation is the means and mass participation is the end, the mass media are useful to the extent that they share information on food, clothing, and shelter with populations in remote areas that is necessary for their education and participation in discussion on these issues. Today, few states are using any mass media to counteract the range of actors and factors that perpetuate underdevelopment and national dependency in the Third World. There is hardly any consistent use of media channels to undo the damage that colonization caused to the self-concept, culture, political structures, and economies of Asia, Africa, the Caribbean, the Middle East, and Latin America.[27] It is difficult to point to any state in the South which has been using the mass media consistently over time as part of its strategy to reduce economic and cultural dependency on First World actors such as transnational corporations and international lending agencies. Hardly any state is using the media to question the legitimacy of internal domination by particular ethnic, caste, and capital-owning groups that suppress the productivity and identity of their majorities. Though politicians' speeches refer to the preceding *causes* of continued underdevelopment, the use of the media for such essential political, cultural, and psychological transformation is rare. One reason for this neglect is that it is not in the interests of the power structure. Another is the limited understanding among economic planners of the conceptual task of redevelopment of these once-developed societies. The challenge is long-term, holistic, and structural. The response, unfortunately, is limited to short-term, symptomatic, and sectoral partial interventions. Separate projects and project bureaucracies are designed to meet different needs of the same person through separate short-term plans. Thus, media use is conceptualized in terms of separate ameliorative project-support applications of 'promotional messages' to deal with hunger, illiteracy, or illness (*symptoms* of underdevelopment) while neglecting the long-term, broadly reeducational attempts needed to eradicate their common *structural root causes*. Practical tips on agriculture, health, and nutrition can correct misinformation. Science broadcasts produced centrally by the best scientists are beneficial. But several good communication interventions that respond to *parts* of the problem do not accumulate to change the underlying *causes* of the larger problem.

The primary question should always be: *who* will benefit from this knowledge, and will the *pattern* of benefits change present unequal relations or not.

Mass media systems in Africa and South Asia are presently organized to send development messages from supposedly know-it-all development experts in capital cities to supposedly ignorant peasants and slum dwellers who are perceived to need develop-ment. This top-down structure of development initiative and its parallel centralized media system reflect the national power struc-ture: the source of development initiatives is at the top, the receivers wait at the bottom quietly, socialized into a 'culture of silence'. The benefits of development trickle down to them occasionally. They are not involved in planning for their own growth and well-being. They are *objects* of humanitarianism, just like they were victims of feudalism, colonization, and underdevelopment. Benefits from the development model of economic growth of the 1960s through high tech industrialization and diffusion of infor-mation accrued to those that have. Hunger, malnutrition, and unemployment continued for the have-nots, in essence, dehumani-zation. The few rich grew richer and the poor remained poor.

Prescriptions from the diffusion model researched in more than 3,000 studies in the Third World did not redress the unequal distribution of wealth in the South that was so different from the US Midwest where the model was developed. Gramsci's sixty-year old insights that truly transformational efforts must include creation of an alternative world view and culture, *alongside and inseparable from* changes in inequitable socioeconomic and political power structures remained unread.[28] Information provi-sion was not coupled with structural change as Gramsci recom-mended. The rich continued to be the most innovative because they had disproportionate access to education, purchasing power, and contacts required for adoption of new ideas. The typical Third

World state did not provide prerequisites for adoption of innovations (e.g., land redistribution as in Korea, Taiwan, and Japan) for the poor majority, preceding or accompanying media messages on improved agricultural, health, education, and family planning practices. 'Development communication' applications were unable to promote significant improvements in the quality of life of individuals and groups within a nation, since they were not planned as part of structural change attempts, and frequently represented escapes from the more difficult (but essential) structural changes required.[29]

Without simultaneous provision of opportunities to act on information presented in media programs, audiences began to *recognize* official development communication programs for what they are—poorly thought out half-gestures without a supportive implementation infrastructure on the ground, or worse, cosmetic attempts to fool the masses into thinking that the ruling party really cared about them.

Grass roots-based, people-centered participatory development strategies that emerged in the 1970s proposed a completely different notion of cultural change distinct from the West to East diffusion of modern ideas via the mass media suggested by well-intentioned US academics. The Brazilian educator Paulo Freire outlined a new methodology that had illiterate adults participating actively in the transformation of their world. He wrote, 'To surmount the situation of oppression, men [*sic*] must first critically recognize its causes, so that through transforming action they can create a new situation, one which makes possible the pursuit of a fuller humanity...a pedagogy must be forged *with*, *for*, the oppressed in the incessant struggle to regain their humanity.'[30] The internal political structure of Third World states constrains implementation of Freire's pedagogy. But, the mass media can *potentially* trigger the individual reflection and horizontal discussion required within communities for collective action to transform an oppressive world.

In Freire's proposed pedagogy of the oppressed, the teacher (or media producer) is no longer the authority, but a learner-cum-teacher: someone who both learns and teaches *in dialogue* with other fellow learners-teachers. The dialogue-based message design process proposed in this book tries to *approximate* the Freirean ideal: media producers and media audiences teach each other through mandatory preproduction and midproduction dialogues.

Media producers listen and observe first, and then present draft messages (story boards, scripts, photographs) to the community to validate whether they conform to their needs and customs. Thus, a dialogue with a group, representative of the larger community, precedes the design of mediated messages for discussion by the masses that the producer cannot see or hear individually. This does not provide the dialogue-based learning and teaching opportunity *for all* that is quintessentially Freirean, but it uses Freirean methods to establish the relevance of message topics and formats through dialogue with a representative sample of the audience. This is an opportunity for bottom-up intervention in the media power structure that cannot be ignored. The danger is that the power structure will instruct media producers to use this methodology to package *their* agenda in the terminology of the people. Such cosmetic attempts work in some kinds of advertising communication but cannot lead to the informed participation required for self-sustaining national development.

While relevance to the *masses* was of concern to both Gramsci and Freire, neither wanted to exclude the ideas of the ruling elite, property owners, and traders. While Gramsci opposed abstention from institutions of the ruling class (e.g., producers and researchers who do not want to be co-opted by commercial media organizations, state television stations, or the Ministry of Commerce and Industry) as a form of infantile leftist dogmatism, Freire sees the need for mutual humanization and liberation for both the teacher-learner (read media production team) and the learner-teacher (read audience). No national consensus or individual change can take place without *dialogue*:

(a) within groups of people with homogeneous needs,
(b) between groups of people with different needs, and
(c) between the public and planners (e.g., government agencies, private voluntary organizations) claiming to meet their needs.

This implies horizontal communication within and between groups in which people are organized (e.g., women's groups, caste groups, religious groups). This implies vertical, bottom-up, people-to-planner information flows on needs, priorities, and preferred modes of meeting them. And it also includes top-down, planner-to-people information flows in response to community information they receive. Information has to keep flowing three ways in a never-ending spiral as it were, first horizontally and then up, and then back down, continuously, and on a variety of issues. The dialogue at each loop or circle of the spiral may sometimes lead to communication, i.e., a sharing of meaning, and sometimes it may not. But the spiral-shaped system must keep information flowing constantly if national development is to be broad-based and self-sustaining.

The dominant form of information flow in most nations is top-down. Findings from media effects researches in such contexts are summarized in Chapter 5; they might have lessons for national transformation. For consensus development at the grass roots level, horizontal communication comes first. This is where small, low-cost media can contribute. These decentralized local and regional media production centers are also required to convey the community's consensus upwards. Community communication is the basis of 'communication popular' (people's communication) initiated by peasant and worker organizations in Latin America. Their process is Freirean reflection and action, their direction is horizontal, their leadership is internal, and their end is an equitable economic and social whole in which the individual is an active subject.[31] Attempts to approximate this 'alternative' ideal include monthly newspapers with questions for group discussion followed by publication of answers, radio schools with animators to stimulate discussion, television clubs, theater, sound slides, puppets, posters, the circulation of audio cassettes (recorded on one side and blank on the other for the community to record their suggestions) between organized groups, *fotomontage*, and video tapes to trigger reflection and action.[32, 33, 34] Brazil probably has the largest number of workers' unions and neighborhood groups (over 100) using video, with its own Association of Video in Grass Roots Movements and a Catalogue of Grass Roots Video Program. A bimonthly bulletin called *Video Popular* prints over 2,000 copies. Since 1966, the Metalworkers Union in the chief industrial area of the country has pioneered a *Worker's TV* project for worker training, documentation of events, cultural expression, and as a support for the trade union and grass roots movement.[35]

In 1967, the National Film Board of Canada's *Challenge for Change Programme* (CCP) pioneered the use of film and video in poor remote communities in collaboration with the Memorial University of Newfoundland. CCP produced twenty-six candid film modules on Fogo Islanders in Newfoundland talking about their concerns and interests. When Fogo Islanders watched the films with their community development extension worker, they recognized the value of their knowledge, skills, and lifestyle. They also saw how they were divided among themselves. The 'Fogo process', *linked* to a sustained program of community development led to consensus development and action among the Islanders. It also helped distant government decision makers understand the people and respect their preference for continuing to live where they were. Soon, video substituted for film. Video began to be used for conflict resolution among adversaries reluctant to confront each other, for peer teaching, and to assess and respond to community needs. The Fogo Island process of video for human resource development was successfully tried, under Memorial University supervision, by dairy extension workers in Karnal, India, and by field educators in a women's rural development project in Nepal.[36]

Note that participatory communication can be 'directed' to a particular end, or be open-ended and nondirective.[37] It is directed when it is used by government development projects, commercial marketing agencies and others to help achieve their preestablished goals (e.g. sales of perfume, increased production of high-yielding varieties of rice). 'Directed' participation in message design, message production, and message consumption is an attempt at manipulation of the audience to meet someone else's ends. The power structure and context remain the same; participatory communication is just a more efficient and effective means to the end. An illustration of *directed* participation of audiences in message design is market research by advertising agencies. The goal is sales promotion. Audience input is restricted to selection of content and form that will achieve this end.

Participatory communication to mobilize open-ended self-expression and self-management for self-development is what UNESCO intended in its first seminar on the subject in 1978. Participatory communication was defined as *the social process in which groups with common interests jointly construct a message oriented to the improvement of their existential situation and to the change of the unjust social structure.*[38] Such uses of the media allow communities to break out of the culture of silence and produce early warnings to the ruling party of popular discontent they should redress before they threaten the legitimacy and survival of the state.

Nevertheless, nongovernmental organizations, popular movements, and their communication staff have to proceed cautiously, taking two steps forward and, sometimes, one step backward. Unwelcome protests in one part of a nation that are not orchestrated with like-minded groups across the nation are easily isolated and squashed. National transformational attempts in postcolonial states that are initiated by popular movements must strategically look for the right time and right place to maneuver in the power structure. Media support for social, economic, and political protests have to be orchestrated carefully with other transformational elements to be effective. When social and political conditions were ripe in Iran, audio cassettes of Ayatollah Khomenini's speeches and telephone calls from exile helped fan the resistance against the Shah.

What can government media producers assigned to the sectors of agriculture, health, or education do for national transformation? Their major contribution would be to initiate dialogue with the audience community to verify whether the goals they are assigned are consonant with community needs. When community needs are distinct, it is necessary for media producers to find non-confrontationist ways of communicating the distinct reality (learned from audience dialogue) to those in charge. Since observations of those in power get most media attention, media producers could make it a point to feature the contradictory needs of the masses which are rarely heard. Given the dominance of state-initiated development and development communication initiatives, consistent long-term, low-key attempts by media production teams to re-define 'assigned topics' in light of audience dialogue-based reality ostensibly *for the sake of communication efficiency and effectiveness* would be a significant contribution. Appeals to data generated by a mainstream methodology (preproduction and midproduction audience research) tend to be less threatening than calls for national revolution to redistribute the wealth.

The media are means. They can be used to repress or emancipate. *Media messages are influenced by (but not mechanically reflective of) the interests of those who own and/or control the channels.* The surrounding economic and political context, and the role of the media institution determine the rules and practices which govern the behavior of free-lance and full-time media workers. In spite of identical national rules, the differences in the political content and aesthetic quality of the output of different regional media units speaks for the scope for individual media producers to use their skills to mobilize audiences.

On the face of it, many people see newspapers, radio, and television as owned and primarily financed by the state, private advertisers, license fees, and subscriptions in rare cases. Where does the state get its finances? From taxes paid by the public, surely. How do advertisers finance their advertising? From the prices that the purchasing public pay for their products. Clearly, then, ultimately audiences finance the media of information transmission. The managers and staff of newspapers, radio stations, and television stations are salaried employees of the state, public corporations, or private companies. The concept of the citizen as ultimate financier (and hence their employer and boss) is not something media producers in public service agencies are conscious of.

Nonprofit media units are constrained by their sources of funds and the ideologies of their funding sources. Profit-making media entities (run by the state or private firms) make their money from renting the eyes and ears of the audience to advertisers. The more readers, the more listeners and viewers for a particular program, time-slot, or page, the higher the advertising rates the media channel can charge. They prefer features and programs that attract the largest numbers; controversial programs that risk upsetting (and losing) any part of the audience are rare. Irrespective of whether it is the state or a private corporation that controls for-profit media, the fact is that the audience community's involvement is limited to informing audience researchers how to design entertainment programs and advertisements that will appeal to more of them.

The media are the site where ideologies are produced and reproduced. Whether the state controls the media directly through ownership as in Asia, Africa, and parts of the Caribbean, or indirectly through regulation and advertising support, the fact is that media channels are educational and cultural arms of the state. The economic and political system needs their help to continue. Thus, so-called 'development support media' may actually function in support of the development of the interests of the ruling political and economic powers, and hence their continued dominance rather than as engines of equality and democracy. As state weaponry, the media generally perform several jobs for the state. They produce public consent to state policies; they produce a cultural climate that supports continued accumulation of capital by the ruling classes; they make the present distribution of power (economic, political, and cultural) legitimate by presenting the good parts. The room to maneuver and the opportunity to use these media for change in spite of direct and indirect state control arises because of the conflict between these different functions of the state. To illustrate: most state policies give lip service to human rights, local cultures, and historical tradition. Media programs that celebrate these policies are contradicted by other media programs that show the state running rough-shod over the rights of individuals and the cultural identities of regions that want greater power than the political center is willing to give. Media programs that celebrate government programs to eradicate poverty run simultaneously with media programs laden with capital-intensive high tech suggestions for improvements that cannot be adopted by typical small farmers. Many media producers— full-time employees and supposed 'independent free-lancers'—are not aware of the role that their overt and covert messages play in maintaining and reproducing class, caste, and race distinctions in our societies. However, there are enough cases of journalists, film-makers, videographers, and graphic artists who pioneer alternative communication systems within and outside bureaucracies to give the lie to cynicism and hopelessness. The reduction in the price of printing presses, mimeo machines, sound-slide projectors, and mini-cameras and their increasing portability make it possible for larger numbers of grass roots organizations—trade unions, health agencies, religious groups—to use communication technology and develop an oppositional consensus in their constituencies, and then network with like-minded groups.

The audience participation-based approach to media production and message design is a strategy that enables media workers to use their tools to give diverse audiences a voice in deciding the kind of national transformation they want, distinct from reproducing the present economic and political structure. The more frequent the oppositional voices, the greater is the pressure for the state to change in the interests of its own legitimacy and the capital accumulation needs of the dominant economic power it represents.

Chapter 2 reinstates the audience as the heart of the process of 'mass communication'.

Notes and References

1. The Appendix in this book is a selected bibliography on the mass media and national development.

2. Joan M. Nelson, ed. *Economic Crisis and Policy Choice: The Politics of Adjustment in the Thirld World*. Princeton: New Jersey, 1990.

3. South Commission. *The Challenge to the South*. New York: Oxford University Press, 1990.

4. Latin American scholars played a critical role in the transformation of our understanding of development. The 'dependency theory' was thus generated in the less developed world and diffused to the developed West—rather than the reverse. The founding statement of the dependency approach was written in Spanish in 1969 and translated into English in 1979. It is by F.H. Cardoso and E. Faletto.*Dependency and Development in Latin America*. Berkeley: University of California Press, 1979. Other Third World contributors to this literature include Norman Girvan from the Caribbean and Samir Amin from West Africa. Latin scholars who have written in English on communication aspects of dependency include S. Luis Ramiro Beltran. 'Alien Promises, Objects and Methods in Latin American Communication Research'. *Communication Research*, vol. 3, 2, April 1976, and more recently Omar Souki Oliveira. 'Media and Dependency: A View from Latin America'. *Media Development*, 1, 1989.

5. I. Wallerstein. *The Modern World System: Capitalist Agriculture and the Origins of the European World Economy in the Sixteenth Century*. New York: Academic Press, 1979.

6. Robert C. Bach. 'On the Holism of a World System Perspective', in Terence K. Hopkins and I. Wallerstein, eds., *Processes of the World System*. Beverly Hills: Sage, 1980, pp. 297-301.

7. Everett M. Rogers. *Communication and Development: Critical Perspectives*. Beverly Hills: Sage, 1982.

8. M.N. Srinivas. *Caste in Modern India and Other Essays*. Bombay: Asia Publishing House, 1965.

9. United Nations Development Program. *Human Development Report 1990*. New York: Oxford University Press, 1990.

10. Gita Sen and Caren Grown. *Development, Crises, and Alternative Visions*. New York: Monthly Review Press, 1987.

11. Jan Servaes. *One World, Multiple Cultures*. Leuven: ACCO, 1989.

12. L. Athusser. *Lenin and Philosophy and Other Essays*. London: NLB, 1971, pp. 121-73.

13. Daniel Lerner. *The Passing of Traditional Society*. Glencoe, Illinois: The Free Press, 1958.

14. UNESCO. 'Mass Media in Developing Countries'. *Reports and Papers in Mass Communication*, no. 33, 1961. Paris: UNESCO

15. Lucian Pye, ed. *Communications and Political Development*. Princeton, New Jersey: Princeton University Press, 1963.

16. David McClelland. *The Achieving Society*. New York: Van Nostrand, 1961.

17. Wilbur Schramm. *Mass Media and National Development*. Stanford, California: Stanford University Press, 1964.

18. Everett M. Rogers. *Diffusion of Innovations*. New York: The Free Press, 1983.

19. W.W. Rostow. *The Stages of Economic Growth: A Non-Communist Manifesto*. Cambridge: Cambridge University Press, 1960.

20. A. Eugene Havens. 'Methodological Issues in the Study of Development', *Sociologia Ruralis*, 12, 1972.

21. Everett M. Rogers with L. Svenning. *Modernization Among Peasants: The Impact of Communications*. New York: Holt, Reinhart and Winston, 1969.

22. IIEP. *New Educational Media in Action: Case Studies for Planners*. Vols. 1–3. Paris: UNESCO, 1967.

23. IIEP. *The New Media: Memo to Educational Planners*. Paris: UNESCO, 1967.

24. World Bank. *Radio for Education and Development: Case Studies*. Vols. 1 and 2. Washington, DC, 1977.

25. Dean T. Jamison and Emile G. McAnany. *Radio for Education and Development*. Beverly Hills: Sage, 1977.

26. See Godwin Chu and Wilbur Schramm. *Learning from Television: What The Research Says*. Stanford, California: Institute for Communication Research, 1967.

27. See Walter Rodney. *How Europe Underdeveloped Africa*. Washington, DC: Howard University Press, 1974 and R.P. Dutt. *The Problem of India*. New York: International Publishers, 1943.

28. Quintin Hoare and Geoffrey Nowell-Smith, eds. *Selections from the Prison Notebooks of Antonio Gramsci*. London: Lawrence and Wishart, 1971.

29. Bella Mody. 'From Communication Effects to Communication Contexts'. *Media Development*, 3, 1988.

30. Paulo Freire. *Pedagogy of the Oppressed*. New York: Herder and Herder, 1971.

31. 'Editorial'. *Media Development*, 27, 1, 1980.

32. Jose Martinez Terrero. 'Alternative Media in Latin America'. *Media Development*, 27, 1, 1980.

33. Alan O'Connor. 'People's Radio in Latin America—a New Assessment'. *Media Development*, 36, 2. 1989.

34. Jeremiah O'Sullivan-Ryan. 'Participation is the Key to Development'. *Media Development*, 27, 3, 1980.

35. Regina Festa and Luiz Santoro. 'Policies from Below-Alternative Video in Brazil'. *Media Development*, 34, 1, 1987.

36. Tony Williamson. 'The Fogo Process: Development Support Communications in Canada and the Developing World', unpublished paper. Memorial University of Newfoundland, 1988.

37. Juan E. Diaz Bordenave. 'Participation in Communication Systems for Development', unpublished paper. Rio de Janeiro, May 1980.

38. Quoted in Bordenave above, p. 20. Also see Jeremiah O'Sullivan-Ryan and Mario Kaplun. *Communication Methods to Promote Grassroots Participation for an Endogenous Development Process*. Paris: UNESCO, 1979.

THE INVISIBLE AUDIENCE 2

The 'masses' is no definition of an audience. Who can communicate with everyone at once? I can't get through to my boss and my wife in the same tone of voice...and these are people

I see every day. How can one of my radio programs mobilize 300,000 different listeners I cannot see or hear?

What information do farmers need? I don't know. I live in the city. Agriculture experts tell me what farmers should be told, and I design a poster as attractively as I know how.

My job is to get the audience's attention. My tools are words and pictures. When the audience does not understand what I mean to say, it is often because they are pictorially and verbally illiterate. That's their problem, not mine.

These comments were made by employees of public service agencies, governmental and nongovernmental—a television producer, a graphic artist, and a radio producer. More than a few development communication media producers have become like them over the years. They have jobs in big government and inter-governmental United Nations development agencies. They do not work for or with the masses. Theories of national development and community communication do not interest them any more. Their early enthusiasm for changing the world was killed by the bureaucracy. Free-lance media producers who hoped for funding to produce development communications for mass mobilization were few, but their numbers may be increasing as costs of production equipment fall. This book of suggestions is written for both groups of media producers who make their living off 'mass communication'. Professional media production training generally does not 'waste' time dealing with what we should know from common sense: the importance of beginning with the audience in designing messages to actually achieve communication. As members of media audiences themselves, message designers attend to the information that interests them. Is it not reasonable for message designers to find out what their intended audience wants to know and in what form the information will get their attention before they begin to design messages for others? An audience member's position in society and the nature of that society (and economy and culture) influences his/her interests and information needs. Family attitudes, schools, religion, economic status, individual cultural identity, political power, and present workloads are some of the forces that determine which information audience members attend to. Such factors determine the nature of the barriers and filters that individual audience members use to protect themselves from being overloaded with unwanted information.

How to produce *communication*, as against messages, programs, and artwork? Public service departments in governmental and nongovernmental organizations leave it to media producers and subject experts. Media producers focus on form, technical specialists focus on content. What process is responsible for ensuring that the unique combination of form and content in each message results in effective communication with its intended audience?

Production Values

Quite naturally, mass media designers are proficient in the use of microphones, cameras, or brushes: the tools of the media production trade. Mass media messages are their products. Posters or records that have high production value qualify for awards from fellow artists—for their form and appearance. Therefore, poor lighting, poor illustrations, or a noisy sound track would rightly be considered embarrassments from the production point of view. Is it not embarrassing, too, if a poster gets an award for high production value but is not comprehensible to its readers?

Technical Accuracy

Specialists in agriculture, health, education, and family planning agencies use the media to extend their reach to invisible clientele in remote areas. Traditional educators are rightly concerned about the currentness and technical accuracy of the topics they present. This is their area of responsibility in the program development process. What should a development communicator think of an agricultural television program for farmers that presents the latest capital-intensive technical know-how (unaffordable to the typical low income audience) in textbook language that the audience cannot comprehend? Fellow experts may award it the prize for the best television program on that topic. But, is it not embarrassing that the program disregards what the farm audience wants to know, and how those farmers process information?

Audience Responsiveness

How about the impact of the message from the audience community's viewpoint? Well-intentioned governmental and non-governmental agencies pride themselves on knowing what is good for their publics. They frequently commission media programs to reach out to the masses with their wisdom. The media producer is urged merely to 'sugarcoat' the information. Learn from Madison Avenue, she/he is exhorted. No attempt is made to find out whether the audience wants information on this topic, and if they do not, the reason why. How can the most glamorous big-budget presentation serve the public's needs under such message design conditions?

Community versus Audience

Media technology has the capability to bridge geographical distances between message senders and message receivers who are physi-cally separated from each other. Technological determinists believed that *use* of the technology would guarantee that poor communities would begin to live better as a result of information capsules distributed expeditiously through communication pipe-lines covering the country. The development of television pipe-lines, radio pipelines, print pipelines, and satellite systems (with the development of as many audiences) was seen as a fast, low-cost shortcut or 'leapfrog'. Such methods seemed preferable to the labor-intensive, time-consuming job of visiting each community to resolve their problems. This was a mistake. The media are channels for information delivery; the availability of such hard-ware does not guarantee that the information delivered gives audiences what they need, when they need it, and in the form they need it. Quite often, the problem of the audience is a material resource problem or a political organization problem rather than a lack of information problem.

Nevertheless, the development of a mass media infrastructure ensured that problematic communities would remain unproblematically invisible—by trivializing them into media audiences *(segments* of communities) whose problems were amenable to solution through packages of information. This long-distance, top-down approach to problem resolution through the mass media is a technological attempt to bridge physical distances. It is a good beginning, but, alone, it could not and did not lead either to communication or to national development anywhere [1] Chapter 1 looked at the use of the media for national development. The rest of this chapter and the next analyze the nature of communication.

Producing Communication

Achieving communication is not easy. But it would be impossible to continue as a truly human community, without approximating it, without understanding each other, however imperfectly. The fact is that we *do* successfully approximate communication in conversations and group discussions much of the time. Our task, then, is to understand how, why, and when we succeed, so that we can do the right things more often. In large representative democracies, where decisions cannot be made in face-to-face meetings (as they are in Swiss cantons), finding ways to share meaning across long distances is essential. The public has to make decisions on who should represent them and let their representatives know their concerns. Farmers have to decide what crops they will grow, whether they will boil their water, when it is acceptable to cut down their forests, and how they can protect themselves when employers exploit them. How can we use technological communication pipelines to approximate dialogue—that is, achieve a sharing of meaning among their users, both senders and receivers?

Let us begin with the word *'communication'* itself. When we talk about approximating or achieving communication, we are using the word to refer to an outcome or end-effect. Another use of the term refers to the process. The word 'communication' comes from the Latin *'communis'*, that is, 'common'. The word 'community' comes from the same Latin word. The aim of 'communication' as an outcome is to 'make common', to share. Communication is achieved, then, when the sender and the receiver hold meaning in common, that is, when the meaning the sender wanted to share is identical ('isomorphic' with) to the meaning the audience receives. Under what conditions can such 'communication' take place? *The degree of communication achieved is a function of the relevance of the topic to a particular audience and the appropriateness of the treatment/ presentation/form of the information (i.e., to what degree it facilitates processing by the audience).* Every moment of the day human senders *and* receivers of messages make decisions pertaining to what they will pay attention. This may sometimes be subconscious. At other times, the decision may be a conscious one. Humans set up barriers and filters to protect themselves from being overwhelmed by too much information and to exclude information that would be dissonant with their worldviews and thus disturb their cognitive equilibrium.

Approximating Dialogue

National transformation frequently involves changing old ways— for landlords and the landless, for the haves and the have-nots. How should designers of messages deal with human resistance to new information that calls for a change in old ways? How can a media production team maneuver around the different filters when the audience is invisible? Speakers involved in a conversation or addressing a meeting have direct contact with their audience. They can see/hear the reactions and resistances of those they are addressing and can adjust their words and gestures accordingly. The inter-personal process of communication is basically represented by the following, where S is the **Sender**, M is the **Message**, and R is the **Receiver**:

$$\overset{\rightarrow}{\underset{\leftarrow}{S}} \overset{\rightarrow}{\underset{\leftarrow}{M}} R$$

Persons who are visible and/or audible to each other (or both) can take turns at being sender or receiver as they converse. The arrows going both ways show that the sender and receiver can modify the message until it conveys the meaning they intended. But, with the introduction of mass media (print, radio, television, and film), which help us to physically reach more people simultaneously (the magical multiplier effect), all audiences are beyond the producer-sender's eyesight and earshot. In such technologically mediated communication, via audio cassettes, radio, television, video cassettes, mimeographed or printed matter, the process begins with the sender and ends with the distribution of information through some media channel, as illustrated in the following:

$$\text{Sender} \rightarrow \text{Message} \rightarrow \text{Channel} \rightarrow \text{?}$$

Where are the receivers at the other end of the channel? The audience is visually invisible and unknown, except when an occasional field visit or an audience research study discovers them. Most media production organizations do not guarantee message reception or comprehension because of the structural difference in the interpersonal and mediated information transmission process: senders of technologically-mediated messages do not have the opportunity to personally interact with their audiences and to fine-tune a message so as to facilitate the sharing of meaning. Often, such senders do not know whether there are any receivers at all, who they are, or what meaning they receive from the messages.

Technological Separation

Agriculture, health, and community development agencies and the message producers who work for them are *distanced* from their audiences by the technology they use, in one sense. But they are also *potentially connected* to them through this technological delivery system. This book proposes a methodology to bridge the economic, political, and cultural distance between senders and representative receivers before and during mass media message design. This methodology makes it possible to share meaning, rather than to merely deliver radio programs, flip charts, and audio cassettes as information commodities. Subsequent chapters deal with this in depth.

Bridging the Distance

The audience is invisible. Farmers, traders, industrial workers, mothers, fathers, and children in villages and towns around the world are busy, active people who go about their lives making decisions in their own unique fashions, using whatever relevant information is available. They are not waiting for the next information transfusion from radio, television, or print media to decide how to live their daily lives.

Systematic research has helped us to develop communication hardware (e.g., transistor radios, satellite dishes, mimeograph and photocopy machines) to carry messages to homes and schools in distant rural areas. How can systematic research now help us to develop software (i.e., print and electronic media programs) that can actually provide information in a manner that is responsive to who needs to know what, in which form, at what time, through which channels?

> Once you have ascertained a specific viewer need or desire, you work backwards from viewer experience to what the medium requires in order to produce such an experience.

This advice comes from Herbert Zettl[2], TV producer, aesthetics professor, international consultant, and writer of production texts— not from an audience researcher. Given the spatial distance between the producer and the audience in mass-mediated communication situations, how should a graphic artist or producer of audio cassettes establish the nature of the viewer's needs and produce a viewer experience that meets those needs? What action can the media producer take before and during program production to reduce the risk of producing materials that do not really communicate?

We need to systematically understand audience preferences in terms of topic and treatment. For the information delivery system to achieve communication with its audiences, the message production process must begin with audience-sender dialogue. Media producers must first listen to representative samples of the larger audience specify *their* topic and treatment preferences.

Listening

The basis of the audience dialogue-based methodology is to listen first, and then speak. Listen more, talk less. This is not modern mass communication wisdom derived from years of research. It is folk wisdom. It has also become standard operating procedure in designing commercially-driven marketing communication attempts. Private, profit-making advertising agencies could lose a client or a lot of money if their information campaigns failed to communicate. Unfortunately, government bureaucracies, which are primarily responsible for media mobilization for national development, rarely go out of business irrespective of their performance; ruling parties and persons may change, but the same civil servants with the same insensitivity to public needs continue for the most part.

The proposed communication design process begins with the audience and ends with the audience, as in the following illustration:

The mass communication media are channels that could potentially distribute information packages to large numbers of people. Whether the packages reach the intended audience, whether the receivers find the packages appealing enough to open, and whether the information inside is digestible will depend upon whether the information packagers (writers, graphic artists, radio producers) know what attracts audience attention—what information that particular audience is hungry for.

Chapter 1 presented an overview of the origins and nature of communication use for national development in the Third World. Chapter 3 introduces the audience participation-based message design approach.

Notes and References

1.   E.M. Rogers. *Communication and Development: Critical Perspectives*. Newbury Park: Sage, 1976.
2.   Herbert Zettl. *TV Production Handbook*. Belmont: Wadsworth, 1984, fourth edition.

AUDIENCE PARTICIPATION-BASED MESSAGE DESIGN: THE IDEA 3

S ince the early 1970s, development researchers have pointed out that the lack of 'results' has been due to a lack of 'popular participation'. Despite advances in computer and telecommunication technology that make two-way interaction a possibility, most media continue to be hierarchically dominated, centrally controlled, one-way, top-down channels for information dissemination. They are programed by professional producers to meet the needs of the government and advertisers rather than their audience communities. The oligopoly of power (the state, foreign capital, and local capital) is reflected in an oligopoly of information; this leads to an antidemocratic, technócratically induced silence. How can democracy be introduced into the relationship between sender and receiver? Many productions are based on the producer's instincts or on the expert's technical knowledge of the subject of the message. The outcome is primarily a product of the interplay between the two. Thus, audience participation is a marginal factor. This chapter presents a method for incorporating audience participation into the *design* of development communication. In communication terms, *this audience-based approach implies making the audience the sender or source of the message as well as the receiver.* The communication process is transformed from a linear, one-way, sender-to-receiver monologue to a circular dialogue, where representative members of the audience reach out to the production team, who then reach out to all other members of the audience.

A close-up shot of a mosquito in a film on malaria is not recognized as a mosquito. Villagers announce that they don't have such big creatures in their area, so they have nothing to fear from malaria. Why? Because producers used the grammar of cinema that *they* were trained to use, not what the audience can understand.

A radio program tells coffee farmers how to prune their bushes in a way that will increase productivity, in the long run. Having been in coffee farming for generations, the farmers already know how to prune their bushes. Their problem is not lack of information, it is lack of resources. They are reluctant to adopt this useful practice because they are small farmers who do not have savings to support them during several seasons when the recently-pruned bushes will produce little. The program was based on what the coffee expert (subject specialist) thought the audience needed to know.

These often-repeated failures in achieving communication

could be avoided, if the audience provided the basis for *what* to communicate, and *how* to communicate. Could preproduction visits to the audience have told production planners about their receivers' unfamiliarity with film conventions? Could audience testing of the story board or rough cuts of the malaria film have told the film editor that close-ups, flashbacks, and flash-forwards should be used with caution? Could the coffee expert advising the production team have visited low-income coffee farmers to find out what they knew about coffee farming before assuming that their failure to practice pruning resulted from a lack of information? The common element in all these situations is the fact that production planners— media workers and subject specialists—could have avoided expensive mistakes by making preproduction visits to the audience community. What would we say about physicians who prescribed medicine without examining their patients? Are development communication media producers doing something similar as they work to promote the health of their nations?

Our everyday experience tells us it is impossible to reach an understanding with another person without using back-and-forth conversation to clarify issues as we deconstruct (breakdown) and then construct *meaning* from each other's messages. Habermas[1] points out that understanding is based on interaction and discourse where all parties have equal opportunity to explain, interpret, and justify without fear, violence, or sanctions. Only under such circumstances will a consensus based on the best argument emerge. How is it possible to achieve an identity of meaning through the vertical, top-down, one-way dissemination of information to a media audience that is perforce mute, because the state chooses not to pay for the installation of a technology that offers two-way communication capabilities for remote areas? How can we capture some of the horizontal, back-and-forth interaction that helps to approach a sharing of meaning in interpersonal communication?

RESOURCING THE AUDIENCE

Despite the power differences inherent in economic, political, and cultural status, senders and receivers are equal partners in the construction of meaning. To paraphrase a popular expression: **Meaning Lies in the Mind of the Receiver**. The media technology that seeks to deliver information to distant places cannot promise communication. Sender-receiver dialogue can improve its chances. It seems reasonable to schedule time and money for such a conversation in the message planning phase. Media production skills have their place, but to put them *first* is to mistake the lesser (talking) for the greater (listening). A manageable number of typical members of audience segments must be sampled systematically as *sources* of information on what they want to see and hear and in what form, with the media production team as information receivers. This will enable the mass media production team, normally deprived of interaction with the media audience, to acquaint themselves with the range of information that is required.

The Audience as Sender

The reader of this book is no more an empty vessel waiting to be filled with new information than is the village audience of radio and television programs. As the reader of this book has had life experiences that differ from those of the author, so audiences of other media will have current lifestyles, histories, and ways of processing information that differ from those of the message designers who work in those media.

Since Lasswell's, *Who Says What to Whom with What Effect*[2] question, the notion of one-way transmission has characterized most conceptualizations of mediated communication. It cannot be repeated too often that an identity of meaning cannot be achieved between a sender and a receiver unless both have a chance to participate in a dialogue as they construct meaning. Media organizations impose a handicap on their staffs when they do not require their producers to go to small groups of audience members to dialogue about audience needs and preferences before developing posters and programs for distribution. No matter how much money an organization may spend to hire the best trained producers of posters and broadcast programs, no matter how much foreign exchange it may spend to import expensive equipment and trainers, the organization that excludes the audience from the message design process is doomed to being merely an 'information distribution' organization.

It will have no capability to reach an identity of meaning with the audience.

Putting the 'Masses' Back into Communication

In the audience dialogue-based mode of production, the audience, which is mute in the one-way mass media transmission mode, gets invited into the preproduction and midproduction planning processes as a partner. The communicative success of messages designed on this basis then depends on how well the designers of the mediated production *listen* to this source. Unfortunately, listening skills are not ordinarily included in media production training programs.

True, producers and subject specialists in agriculture, health, or education who commission media campaigns have control over what information they distribute. But senders do not control what and how much is *actually* communicated—the receiver does. The more message designers tailor their productions to the information needs of their diverse massive audiences, using the idiom of the audience, the better the chance of communicating (approximating identity of meaning between sender and receiver).

Media message designers who do spend time and energy listening to their audiences' preferences usually work in advertising-financed systems whose revenues are determined by the size of the audience they attract. Revenues earned, (i.e., rupees, pounds, dollars, pesos) seem to be the major motivation that leads conventional for-profit media productions to ensure that their messages are audience-responsive.

Why do media producers in nonprofit public service systems such as agriculture, health, and education pay little attention to whether anybody is listening? Is audience attention and the achievement of an identity of meaning between sender and receiver not important for national transformation, news, public affairs, and agriculture extension? Why are audiences so rarely factored into planning decisions in noncommercial media organizations, when the public good is at stake rather than the profits of private advertisers?

The development message designer working as part of a national transformation campaign must bear in mind the following *audience-related factors* before deciding what to say, to whom, how, and through which media mix: physical exposure of the audience to the selected medium on the day/date it is carrying the message, the sociocultural sensitivity of the topic and its form, the political appropriateness of the content and its treatment, the economic compatibility of the message with, and the psychological appropriateness of the message for, individual audience members.

Physical access to the message is basic in determining one aspect of how to communicate, i.e., what combination of channels to use. Which media will actually '*reach*' the intended audience? Of those media, what percentage of the intended receivers will be reached by each? How '*frequently*' can the budget afford to use this medium, since the chances of getting attention and evoking interest are limited without repetition? Is the primary channel of information delivery selected for this audience actually only a marginal reminder medium for the community? Is the pattern of *timing* of medium usage the most appropriate for this audience's daily work schedule, thus helping to guarantee physical exposure?

There is no point in designing an AIDS prevention media campaign for rural communities that is primarily based on a television delivery system when television does not reach the majority of villagers. This may seem to be an obvious point, but it is frequently ignored when the broadcasting minister, for example, makes such a decision, despite data to the contrary. If radio is used primarily as background to wake up to and dress by, and is not the center of attention at any point in the day (e.g., for news), it too cannot effectively serve as the chief means of information transmission. In such a case, why not think about using television to reach field extension workers in regional headquarters? Interpersonal communication through extension field workers who are like the audience in some ways ('near-peers') could then be the primary medium of information exchange with villagers. The extension worker would be trained to listen first, and then to respond to the receiver's information needs. Audience-appropriate charts, radio spots and posters can supplement the extension worker's interventions.

Sociocultural sensitivity is critical in deciding *what* is communicated and *how* it is communicated, i.e., topics, treatment, and channel selection. This is particularly important when the content is counter-cultural.

Topics such as birth control, abortion, and sexual practices are guaranteed to arouse strong feelings across cultures. They must be approached differently in different cultures. Media attempts to promote equality and freedom of speech for women have run into strong cultural resistance in many areas. Producers of the Indian commercial TV serial *Hum Log* decided to soft-pedal women's issues and family planning as a result of audience resistance rather than risk losing advertising. Patriarchal society is justified in the Hindu culture by the *'pativrata'* ideology which holds that a woman's spiritual salvation depends upon her total devotion, service, and subordination to her husband. In some religions and cultures, a group communication situation such as sitting together around a single radio or television set, may not be considered appropriate for both genders.

The political compatibility of topics, treatment, and media combinations with the organization and distribution of power at various levels in a society is crucial. Few ruling parties, agricultural landowners, industrialists, and religious authorities welcome media messages that undermine their position. When cracks and contradictions between the alliance of these dominant groups emerge, the time is ripe in the apparently impregnable power structure for major transformational attempts.

Economic compatibility of the content with national policy and the purchasing power of the intended audience is important. When state rhetoric on eradicating poverty and redistributing wealth is high, it would be hard to fault grass roots media initiatives in this direction. State media exhortations to small farmers to use capital-intensive technology that they cannot afford are frequent examples of economic incompatability between message and audience.

The psychological appropriateness of message content, form, and channels for individual receivers has received a preponderance of attention in the literature on media effects. The 1989 edition of *Public Communication Campaigns* is a recent summary.[3]

SYSTEMATIC STEPS IN AUDIENCE INVOLVEMENT FOR MESSAGE DESIGN

The production of messages for distribution through the media is an industrial process composed of interrelated steps, just as the mass production of soap or cars is an assembly line process composed of different steps. The goal in development communication is message production in support of the mass mobilization goals of the grass roots organization, the government or the nonprofit group initiating this transformation. This section focuses on the process, viewed as a system of interrelated parts working towards a common goal. The entire system uses feedback to determine if its desired goal is reached, thus enabling it to modify itself according to the results. Why be *systematic* in involving the audience before and during production for national transformation? Those that are aware that audience participation in education, development, and national transformation is a political enterprise seem to be temperamentally averse to using efficient, rational, and systematic methods to achieve their ends. It is as if spontaneous revolution was of the essence; efficiency and process/product rationality seem to be tainted because they have worked too well for dominant groups. The system in power does not rule without a method; any threats will be put down systematically and must therefore be planned logically. Why should producers of media programs bother with listening to and observing audiences, given that media producers are audience members themselves? Why is it not enough to hire a producer who grew up with a particular audience and a content expert who visits them from time to time? Why must audience dialogue visits be scheduled, and monitored to ensure they took place?

Each of us has our own perceptions of places we know, colored by our past experiences and relationships. Our general knowledge of a community is affected by our personal biases. Production planners need unbiased audience dialogue for the foundation of their programs, not general hunches and educated estimates. If those who manufacture soap and cars for mass markets base their product design and advertising decisions on hard data about their consumers, why should public service communicators be less conscientious?

Media production and transmission cost money, time, and skills. The costs are a worthwhile investment only if communication is achieved. Without systematic audience involvement, the results have not been encouraging (see articles by Dervin, McGuire, and Wallach in Rice and Atkin, note 3).

The steps below outline a *systematic* community-centered approach to program development. These steps represent a set of

interconnected elements applicable to all topics, media, and countries. They form a general (or model) system.[4] The amount of time,
money, staff, and creativity allotted to each step may vary, but the
foundation of this systematic approach is an acknowledgment of
the equal partnership of the audience in achieving communication.
Whether the media are state controlled or privately owned, the
audience controls whether or not posters and programs will communicate. Therefore, it is the needs and preferences of the audience
which should dictate how the producer designs media messages. In
production terms, the audience directs the show. A production
team that has the good sense to put the audience in the director's
chair will find the following steps useful:

1. **LEARN EVERYTHING ABOUT THE TOPIC.** The
   topic may have been selected by a foreign funding
   agency, a domestic politician, a civil service bureaucrat,
   or a community organization. It may be a topic you
   picked yourself. You may have an expert on the topic
   available to you, you may have a production assistant
   who is making good use of all available libraries. In some
   cases, you may have no such help. Whatever the situation,
   make sure you have checked your facts so you do not
   mislead and misinform the masses of people who will be
   exposed to your message.

2. **OBSERVE THE LIFESTYLES AND VALUES OF DIF-
   FERENT SEGMENTS OF THE AUDIENCE TO HELP
   YOU DECIDE HOW TO COMMUNICATE.** The large
   numbers reached by a medium will include a range of
   different groups. Which creative-mobilization strategy
   and treatment will best communicate with all of them?
   The media you select; the frequency with which you
   present programs on the topic; the words, gestures,
   characters, and settings you choose; and whether you
   treat the topic in serious, comical, dramatic, or farcical
   form will be determined by the age, sex, race, occupation,
   education, economic class, and religions of the audience
   with whom you aim to share your meaning. To persuade
   teenagers to eat green, leafy vegetables will require a
   different tone and different arguments than those needed
   to persuade mothers. Chapter 8 deals with the details of

Figure 3.1: Steps in Audience Participation-Based Message Design

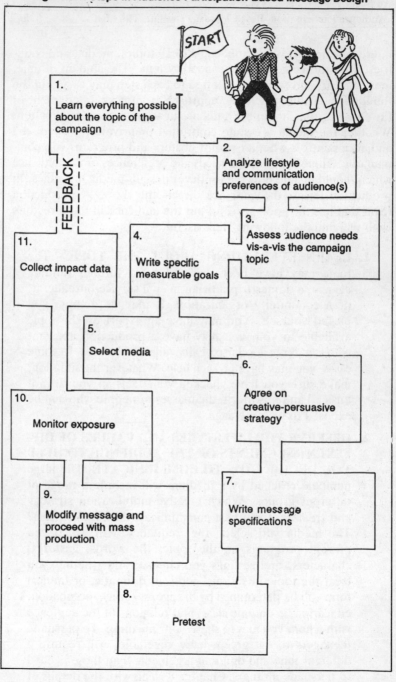

audience segmentation and discusses how to conduct life-style profiles.

3. **DIALOGUE WITH THE AUDIENCE ON WHAT EACH SEGMENT ALREADY KNOWS, FEELS, AND DOES ON THE TOPIC.** Indigenous knowledge is knowledge unique to the audience's culture and society. This is in contrast to the international knowledge or technical knowledge in which subject specialists are trained. Indigenous knowledge speaks of the unique ways in which communities deal with their problems. An astute communication design team will capitalize on what works locally and on what is native to the community, rather than introducing alien concepts, be they Japanese or German. Dialogue on (and document) the audience's present—the knowledge, beliefs, images, misconceptions, legends, attitudes, and behaviors. The entry level or baseline of the typical audience member will determine what to say and how much to say.

4. **WRITE DOWN THE OBJECTIVE: WHAT AUDIENCE IMPACT SHOULD BE USED TO MEASURE WHETHER COMMUNICATION HAS BEEN ACHIEVED?** Given the gap between community base levels and what the community organization or government want to achieve, what can media messages on this topic realistically achieve? This should be the specific objective by which communication effectiveness will be measured with this particular audience community.

5. **CHOOSE WHICH CHANNELS AND WHAT FREQUENCY OF EXPOSURE IS REQUIRED TO REACH THE OBJECTIVE YOU HAVE SET.** Some audience segments pay more attention to the printed media while others restrict themselves to the radio. The mass media do not reach some communities. Some topics are visual topics, some are not. Needless to say, many producers specialize in one medium, or they work in organizations that house only print, radio, television, or film. The question then is: can a specific community group be reached on a specific issue through the medium available? The selection of the mixture of media must be

based on information collected regarding the community group's communication habits and how the group relates to the intended topic. This information then serves as a basis for planning the combination of media.

6. **DESIGN A CREATIVE-PERSUASIVE STRATEGY TO PACKAGE THE MEANINGS YOU WANT TO SHARE.** Development communication designers are frequently housed in departments of agriculture, health, and education. Such departments typically are concerned with the technical accuracy of what they are instructed to share. They do not think enough about *how to communicate*. They fail to ask which format will attract attention, hold attention, and ensure comprehension. An appeal to the community's emotions may work better than a rational appeal to their intellect. Information collected about your audience's media habits and information needs should serve as a guide in selecting the most appropriate presentation style. A statement of strategy is the necessary systematic basis for the next step.

7. **WRITE SPECIFICATIONS FOR EVERY MESSAGE, DESCRIBING ITS GOAL, CONTENT, AND RECOMMENDED FORMAT/TREATMENT.** Consider this a memorandum of agreement on production content and form among all the people working on the design of a message. On one sheet of paper, specify what this message will achieve, what content will go into it, and how this content will be packaged to ensure audience attention and comprehension. The designers of equipment that is supposed to work under specific conditions—radios, televisions, and furniture—have unambiguous 'specs' (specifications) to direct them, and so should you, the designer of media programs. Since no development communication goal is achieved through just one program, write 'specs' for the series of programs planned. Argue with others in the production team about the strengths and weaknesses of various approaches *before* you adopt one approach. The 'specs' are analogous to a curriculum and lesson plans; do not start production until the 'specs' for the series are completed,

outlining how each program will build on every other to reach the larger development communication goal.

8. **PRETEST THE CREATIVE-PERSUASIVE STRATEGY ON A SAMPLE OF THE AUDIENCE TO FIND OUT WHETHER THE CHOSEN APPROACH IS WORK-ING.** Test the concept, story line, characters, sets, first few programs in a series, rough cuts, storyboards, paste-ups, and draft scripts. The purpose is to check how well the production *performs with this audience* on crucial criteria such as attention, comprehension, novelty, utility, and credibility, *before mass production*, when it will be too late to correct such problems. Jokes can fall flat. Punch lines may carry no punch with the *community audience*, even if your spouse thought they were spectacular. Predistribution testing can save your organization from being embarrassed and losing money because of misinformation, misunderstanding, and information loss.

9. **MODIFY THE MESSAGE DESIGN ACCORDING TO PRETEST FINDINGS AND THEN PROCEED WITH FINAL PRODUCTION.** A test of a rough draft of the message on a sample of the audience can provide an early warning that the objective is too ambitious, the format is inappropriate, or the content is too complex. The pretest can also indicate that the audience failed to understand crucial terms in the script. The audience may state that they do not like the title of the program, the faces of the characters, or the sets chosen. This trial run can also indicate that the prescriptions recommended by the content expert are not appropriate for the intended audience. Modify message designs in light of audience reactions. If the writer-producer lets the audience direct his/her creative skills, he/she cannot help but communicate.

Steps 10 and 11 are process evaluation and summative impact evaluation. They complete the systematic approach to message design for development communication. These steps are usually undertaken by a research team that is separate from the formative research/ production team for two reasons: these evaluations require different skills. and the use of a different team of people allows for objectivity that comes with separation from the production process.

10. **MONITOR PHYSICAL EXPOSURE, ATTENTION, COMPREHENSION, AND IMPLEMENTATION LEVELS AFTER MESSAGE DISTRIBUTION BEGINS.** This feedback indicates whether your decisions regarding media, content, and form are working under real world conditions. You must determine whether the technological delivery system of the mass media is carrying the message to its intended audiences. Unless the messages are physically available in reception situations where they have a good chance of being read, heard, or observed, as the case may be, no communication potential exists. And, if the message is available, is it being attended to, comprehended, and used?

11. **EVALUATE WHETHER THE MESSAGE IS ACHIEVING ITS KNOWLEDGE, FEELING, AND BEHAVIOR GOALS.** In *development* communication campaigns, communication is the means, development is the end. A program may communicate perfectly; the sender and the many receivers may get the same meaning out of the message, but the intended goal (e.g., questioning established attitudes and changing behaviors) may not follow. An evaluation of the impact of the program in terms of its development goals is essential. Without this final summative evaluation, the development planner will not know whether this communication campaign was the best means to achieve the development goal, whether a different campaign should be tried next year, or whether the mass media should not be used at all in future years.

Audience Visits

Plan a sequence of two audience visits during the preparatory stages of a program series. The first visit would be to research *what to say* in the series and *how to say* it. This is the needs assessment and audience communication preferences trip. A second visit should be scheduled when a rough program, script, or storyboard is ready to be tested on the audience. This would be the midproduction pretesting trip.

Plan visits to the audience in such a way as to accomplish *several* things on a trip. For example, collect preproduction 'what to say and how to say it' information on *several* new programs or series and conduct midproduction tryouts of several new programs and scripts that are awaiting test and evaluation before they can be finalized. Let production colleagues know when an audience visit is scheduled, so the work of several teams can be tested during the same trip.

If assigned to make programs for women, or children, or farmers, set up separate panels of women, children, or farmers as regular informants so you can go back to them frequently without having to reestablish credentials, as a stranger from the city will have to do with every new group of informants. The more a pretest audience is encouraged to be openly critical during the formative stages of program development, the better the production team protects itself from communication ineffectiveness after distribution.

PARTICIPATORY FORMATIVE EVALUATION

Where do these systematic steps for audience involvement in program planning, design, production, and utilization come from? These simple common sense tips on community involvement in the design of products and services are adapted from a variety of fields—operations research and industrial engineering, educational curriculum development and instructional design, and advertising and marketing.

Evaluation research is defined as the systematic collection and analysis of evidence to aid decision making on the effectiveness and utility of a particular product or service for specific users. This kind of research is designed to facilitate decision making in a specific setting; the findings are not meant to be generalized to production settings in other times or places (although there may be lessons that can be drawn from one situation to another). Stufflebeam[5] demonstrates how one should build such systematic evaluation research into all stages of a project—from defining its *context*, to pretesting the *input*, to monitoring the *process*, to establishing the impact of the finished *product*. It is therefore known as the CIPP approach.

First used by educational researcher Michael Scriven[6] in 1967, then made famous in broadcasting circles by its use in *Sesame Street*, the term *formative evaluation* refers to the systematic collection and analysis of evidence to aid decision making *during* the planning, design, and production stages of a program, product, or system. All that this term really means is making use of audience-impact data from an early version of a program or product to improve the intended impact of its final version. This constitutes community-to-communicator information flow, with the audience community as sender.

Preproduction formative evaluation may be used as an aid to planning, to help decide *what to communicate* in a broad general area (e.g., health) through assessments of the information contexts and information needs of users. Not surprisingly, this stage of formative evaluation is called *context evaluation* by some, *needs assessment* by others, and *diagnostic* research or *front-end research* by still others.

During program design, evaluation research could help provide data on *how to communicate* with a particular audience/user group—which idea or concept, titles, characters, sets, story lines, appeals, and alternative creative strategies will work. This stage is called *input evaluation* by some, and *pretesting* by most.

After distribution of a program series, evaluation research can *monitor* the process of its reception: what proportion of the intended audience was exposed to the program? This stage of evaluation research is frequently called *process evaluation* or process monitoring. Once a program is distributed and received, evaluation research can summarize its impact and compare this with the original goals. This summation of the impact of the whole program is called *impact evaluation*, c *summative evaluation*. Summative evaluation has become a basic feature of modern management, especially in times of shrinking resources.

Tragically, formative research into the development of pioneering program initiatives (to help improve their chances of success) are less frequent. Prominent users of formative research in message design are the US Department of Health's Health Message Testing Service, the Children's Television Workshop in New York, the Agency for Instructional Television in Indiana, and the Open University in the United Kingdom. Prestesting was used heavily in family planning campaigns in the Third World, but without any prior audience analysis of media preferences or audience needs assessments to help select audience-appropriate topics and treatment. The Institute for Mathematical Studies in the Social Sciences undertook one of the most carefully integrated uses of formative evaluation in message design to develop radio programs to teach the primary school math curriculum in Nicaragua. This project was assisted by US foreign aid grants to Stanford University.[7] This methodology has since been used to develop educational materials in USAID projects in other countries, dealing with a variety of topics ranging from agriculture to language teaching. Elsewhere at Stanford University, Everett M. Rogers and Douglas Soloman designed a draft manual on formative evaluation for use in their classes. At the University of Michigan, Jerome Johnstone broadened the 1979 Godwin Chu and Wilbur Schramm[8] book that summarized the research on the subject of learning from television. Funded in part by the Corporation for Public Broadcasting in the United States, he produced a 1987 publication entitled *Electronic Learning*.[9] Illustrations from these works are included in both editions of *Public Communication Campaigns*,[10] and in *Information Campaigns* edited by Charles Salmon.[11] Barbara Flagg's book, *Formative Education for Educational Technologies*,[12] uses case studies to describe the concepts, practices, and methods for developing computer software, television programs, optical discs, and teletext magazines. Social marketing has used some of these audience-based methods to change specific individual behaviors in public health and family planning. The marketing of condoms, foam, contraceptive pills, and oral rehydration therapy (ORT) packets have been handled in Third World countries by governments and private sector research, advertising, and marketing firms in India, Sri Lanka, Thailand, Bangladesh, Kenya, Indonesia, Philippines, Egypt, and Nigeria. Thus, commercial marketing concepts of segmentation, consumer research, idea configuration, communication, facilitation, incentives, and exchange theory have been used to promote public service goals in some cases.

In conventional formative and summative evaluation designs, the program's financiers and managers have a great influence over the scope, methods, and direction of the process. The input of the audience is not invited. Particularly evaluation starts with the stakeholders. This chapter has described the principles of the participatory ideal in message design. Note that real power is given to the community at every step, as against token involvement. The process of message design becomes a collaboration. The next chapter looks at the implementation and ethics of this approach.

Notes and References

1. Jurgen Habermas. *Knowledge and Human Interests*. Boston: Beacon Press, 1971.
2. Harold D. Lasswell. 'The Structure and Function of Communication in Society', in Lyman Bryson, ed. *The Communication of Ideas*. New York: Harper and Brothers, 1948.
3. Ronald E. Rice and Charles K. Atkin, eds. *Public Communication Campaigns*. Newbury Park: Sage, 1989, second edition.
4. Walter Dick and Lou Carey. *The Systematic Design of Instruction*. Glenview, IL.: Scott Foresman and Co., 1985, second edition.
5. D. L. Stufflebeam. 'The CIPP Model for Program Evaluation', in G. F. Madaus, M. S. Scriven, and D. L. Stufflebeam, eds. *Evaluation Models: Viewpoints on Educational and Human Services Evaluation*. Boston: Kluwer-Nijhoff, 1983.
6. Michael Scriven. 'The Methodology of Evaluation', in R. Tyler, R. Gagne, and M. Scriven, eds. *Perspectives of Curriculum Evaluation*. Chicago: Rand McNally, 1967.
7. Barbara Searle, Patrick Suppes, and Jamesine Friend. 'The Nicaragua Radio Math Project'. *Radio for Education and Development*, vol. 1, World Bank Staff Working Paper No. 266, May 1977.
8. Godwin Chu and Wilbur Schramm. *Learning From Television: What the Research Says*. Washington, DC: National Association of Educational Broadcasters, 1979, fourth edition.
9. Jerome Johnstone. *Electronic Learning: From Audiotape to Videodisc*. Hillsdale, NJ: Erlbaum Associates, 1987.
10. Ronald E. Rice and William J. Paisley, eds. *Public Communication Campaigns*. Beverly Hills: Sage, 1981, first edition.
11. Charles T. Salmon. *Information Campaigns: Balancing Social Values and Social Change*. Newbury Park: Sage, 1989.
12. Barbara Flagg. *Formative Evaluation for Educational Technologies*. Hillsdale, NJ: Lawrence Erlbaum Associates, 1990.

AUDIENCE PARTICIPATION-BASED MESSAGE DESIGN: IMPLEMENTATION AND ETHICS 4

Let us assume that there is agreement on the *idea* of systematically collecting and analyzing data to develop community mobilization messages for national transformation. The problem arises when discussion turns to who will do it, how fast, when, and at what cost. The first half of this chapter deals with how to implement the participatory ideal. The second half raises questions about whether this approach should be idealized, and what its problems are.

IMPLEMENTATION

Whether the technologies of information are harnessed to transmit *and* receive, so as to allow audiences to speak *and* listen (as in Bertolt Brecht's vision of emancipatory radio) will ultimately depend on the power structure of the particular society, and the influence of external agencies which impact on the project. Following is an illustrative case from Jamaica.

First, We Listen[1]

Between 1972 and 1980, with Michael Manley as its constitutionally elected Prime Minister, Jamaica attempted to establish a democratic welfare state in the backyard of the United States. It discovered that steering a path between the Cuban revolutionary model and the Puerto Rican model of total dependency on the United States was not easy.

This is the background against which Jamaica tried to use this participatory approach to design a community radio station in the Jamaican countryside to enable farm folk to communicate with each other, from 1979 to 1983.

Radio in Jamaica

Jamaica then had two competitive radio systems—the older and more popular Radio Jamaica-Redifussion (RJR) which is not owned by the government and is completely financed by advertising, and the Jamaican Broadcasting Corporation (JBC) which is wholly owned by the government and is financed by government and advertising revenues. Until 1976, both radio systems originated both AM and FM transmissions from the capital city of Kingston. To remedy complaints of poor reception quality by advertisers who preferred RJR, the JBC decided to introduce regional transmitters that would carry the national program from Kingston, and generate a little local programing for local advertisers. With minimum monthly expenditure limited to a secretary-turned-station manager and disc jockey, the first new regional radio station in the tourist resort of Montego Bay began to attract a lot of local advertising for JBC. The second regional radio station, designed for Jamaica's northeast, was donated by UNESCO since it was proposed that this station would be a pilot project in community radio. How should JBC get a radio station for its Central Jamaica region?

Agriculture Radio in Central Jamaica

In 1977, the British Overseas Development Agency and the University of Sussex invited JBC to attend a conference on development communication in Brighton, England. On his return home, JBC's Director of Public Affairs heard of a large integrated rural development project in Central Jamaica that had been proposed by UNDP and was now being financed by foreign aid provided by the United States Agency for International Development (USAID). The project aimed to increase agricultural production through the adoption of hill-side terracing—but it had no 'communication component' to mobilize farmer participation. So the JBC public affairs director put his new knowledge to work and wrote a proposal for a multimedia interpersonal and mass media strategy for the new project. His proposal included only a small role for the JBC: the production of a few programs to elicit farmer participation in the new agricultural project.

With the need to replace twenty-five year old broadcasting equipment in Kingston and get a radio system for Central Jamaica, JBC's then head sent his shopping list of broadcast hardware to USAID, couched in terms of a radio station that would transmit programs in support of the new Integrated Rural Development project funded by USAID. This inquiry was not motivated by any organizational commitment to development support communication. USAID's Ph.Ds in education and communication in Washington read between the lines and conveyed their skepticism to JBC Kingston and USAID Kingston.

There is some speculation that the local USAID office overruled USAID Washington's very appropriate reservations. Perhaps they hoped to win political and economic influence in the JBC. If JBC had equipment from USAID, they might mute their strident criticism of the United States in the last few years of the Manley era, USAID Kingston hoped. The second hope was that the JBC might be persuaded to adopt the American NTSC 525 line color TV system if it felt obligated to USAID, given that it was then discussing which color system they should adopt. USAID Kingston gambled and, for the most part, won: JBC decided to place orders for American color TV equipment so they could show American programs without hassling with conversion problems. The anti-US rhetoric continued on JBC for the next year at the end of which foreign and domestic factors led to the election of Edward Seaga's Conservative (pro-US) party. The good intentions of Mr. Public Affairs in the national broadcasting corporation were abused by his own employer, and the good intentions of USAID's Washington staff were overruled by USAID Kingston who wanted to curry favor with JBC.

USAID Washington continued to hold JBC Kingston and Jamaica to the formally stated objective of setting up an agriculture-support radio station. They hoped it would be possible for the station to get farmers involved in the agricultural development of the region, in spite of JBC's different intentions. The present author, then coordinating the USAID-supported graduate program in communication and development at Stanford University, was subcontracted by USAID to advise JBC in setting up this station. The rest of this case study focuses on the attempt to make the audience in Central Jamaica the source of their own programing.

The cast of characters includes different divisions of the United States Agency for International Development (USAID), the government-owned Jamaica Broadcasting

Corporation (JBC) under Manley and his Conservative successor Seaga, radio producers committed to rural development, radio producers who wanted to move to the comfortable life of the big city, farmers, and the present author.

The use of community research as a strategic tool to help 'form' the concept of their radio station and determine programs and transmission times was imported from the foreign adviser's experience in rural India. The primary lesson from the satellite experiment in India was the need to give special attention to programing.

What model of communication would ensure that the source presented topics in words and images the audience sought? If identity of meaning between the source and receiver is what communication is, why not make the receiver and the source the same entity? Why not make receivers the source of their own messages? What more noninterventionist and effective a communication model than the Audience as Source of its own messages can be advocated? This community-rooted conceptualization of the structure of the radio station was designed to re-power and empower the community by reappropriating the community's airwaves and forms of cultural expression expropriated by both advertising and government-financed radio systems. Farm families and agencies responsible for their development in Central Jamaica would have their own radio station to talk to each other in tones of voice that suited them, and on issues that they considered important. Production staff provided by JBC would function as community communication facilitators. This was the vision. There was no objection from USAID Washington or Kingston: all they wanted now was project implementation, and guidelines for the replication of any successes the project might have.

Project Implementation

And so to the implementation part of the story. The USAID-Government of Jamaica (GOJ) grant agreement for a three-year project was signed in 1979. Total dollar commitment by USAID was $550,000 to be used exclusively to finance the costs of US goods and services—unless there was a special requirement that merited an application for an exception. The GOJ committed to provide $154,000 in cash and kind for Jamaican staff, floor space and services to run the radio station.

By the time all the contractual paperwork was done and the project was ready for implementation, Manley's Jamaica was in political and economic straits. Oil prices were spiraling.

Tourism was in a slump due to the world recession. The foreign aluminum companies, upset that Manley had indexed the price of Jamaican bauxite to the market price of finished aluminum they received, began cutting back on bauxite mining in Jamaica, and hence laying off Jamaican workers. Talks with the IMF had broken off. And 700 people died in violence between the supporters of the then Conservative Party opposition and the beleaguered Socialist Party then ruling. In this turmoil, given the government ownership of JBC, some of its staff and most of its programing were completely preoccupied with bolstering the sagging support for Manley's People's National Party. The JBC had no money or time to spare for the new regional radio they wanted in Central Jamaica. A farmer's radio station in the rural area was very low priority, especially since it was to be noncommercial, during the life of the USAID agreement, that is.

Having signed the agreement, the USAID bureaucracy wanted to have an implementation time schedule and some activity to report. Their pressure led to JBC nominating a bright young sociology graduate as station manager. Prior to this, the station manager-designate had been presenting mostly music shows on the national radio system. Having selected him and pointed him in the direction of USAID, JBC did not take the time to delegate the necessary power, budget, transport, and other authorizations he needed to do the job. How was he 'to carry water in a basket', he often asked. He did what he could: he set up a local steering committee of sixteen social service agencies in the new station's coverage area to develop connections with institutions it was to support. The possibility of local radio programing they could tailor as their community outreach tool kept the spirits of the steering committee high, even when JBC HQ delayed authorization to initiate any start-up activity. Uncertainty after the defeat of Manley's government, uncertainty about the reorganizations taking place in all government agencies, and the constant delay put the station manager-designate in an impossible situation. He quit. Two years of the project's life had passed and little had happened.

The country had now settled down to a new government. With a little more than a year to go before the project agreement with USAID expired, and most of USAID funds still not utilized, JBC requested an extension of the project agreement. It began ordering equipment. And it appointed a new station manager. A social worker, dramatic actress, and radio producer, she was the reason for the station's burst of inaugural energy.

Advertisements for a small staff of seven were placed: writer-producers, production assistants, a technical operator, secretarial help, and a driver. Job specifications stressed the importance of rural experience. But like the hero of *The Harder They Come*, young Jamaicans are attracted to the city. A job in the 'country' is considered second-rate by both the high school dropout and the university graduate. To recruit staff willing to work in rural areas who met the educational and experience requirements of JBC's personnel office was very difficult.

There was clearly a contradiction between the kinds of community activists this radio station needed, and staff requirements determined by colonial and present-day economic and cultural pressures. The staff finally hired were in their 20s. They would have preferred jobs in the city, and were less than excited about the self-effacing role of community communication facilitator they were assigned. The job would do as a stepping stone and a source of income until something better came along. The senior producer (with a bachelor's degree) pointed out that this station's policy was completely in reverse of everything he had been taught, beginning with the power given to the receiving audience to determine program topics and treatment. What about 'production values'? What would broadcasting professionals think? But the station manager was excited, and her staff were dragged silently and skeptically into an unlearning and reduction process by their boss.

Production Team Concept

An innovation in station staffing structure was the introduction of a production team with joint responsibility to meet the needs of a particular audience segment. Production teams consisting of a content expert, a community researcher and the writer-producer were constituted for major subject areas (e.g., agriculture, health).

The community researcher was the station liaison with the people who lived in the station's coverage area. She was responsible for 'resourcing' the audience who had had no control over what the station transmitted to them before this point. Her ongoing listing of their needs for information would determine program topic. Her ethnographic descriptions of farmer lifestyles, vocabulary, dialect, and folk forms were to determine transmission times and program formats. Very few applied for this research job that involved living in the 'country' and working out in the 'district' (villages). Of the handful of applicants for the job, not a single one met the formal requirements that included a social science research degree. The applicant who was selected had several years of social work experience and was at home with the rural population. Unfortunately, she had never been to college and was very insecure in dealing with producers with degrees. This led to poor credibility with the production crew who were reluctant to act on her representations of the audience's needs. If the educational and economic context of Jamaica did not generate a native, well-trained community researcher willing to live in the villages and accepted by Jamaican radio production crew, was the innovation of social researcher as community representative a contextually inappropriate idea? Since the alternative of direct involvement of the community in designing its own programing was unacceptable to the bureaucracy and the professional producers in the Jamaican broadcasting establishment, was the 'audience as source' an idea whose time had not yet come?

Programing

How did the production crew respond to the agricultural content adviser telling them what subject to deal with, and what farm remedies to present?

The producer assigned to work on the agricultural programs knew nothing about farming and hence found the agricultural adviser invaluable. He was credible because he had many years' experience as an agriculture officer in this region. A very proper member of the landed elite who drove a Rover and spoke British English, the agricultural expert initially tended to dictate what was good for farmers on the basis of his 'years of experience'. After a few instances of being proven wrong in script tests conducted by the community researcher, the agriculture adviser began to accompany her to the village to 'first check with the audience'. Thus, the agricultural programs broadcast by the station were timely tips that the farmers and the Integrated Rural Development project appreciated. The format of the program unimaginatively followed the 'farmer-interview-cum-lecture-by-expert' style because the topic was not one that stimulated the creative juices of the production staff. Nevertheless, an important achievement was that the farmers did set the agenda for the topics that were presented in the agricultural time-slot.

What about community health? Nurses in village health centers visited by the researcher were quite candid about health care needs. Thus, the writer-producer of health programs knew what ailments were coming in for treatment, openly and secretly. She found out what tried-and-true folk remedies and allopathic prescriptions were being used. This data was the basis of two programs: a question-and-answer show with a local doctor, and a village-based drama series set in a village. The radio doctor who talked about cures was selected because of her ability to speak in simple Jamaican English. The dramatic series dealt with prevention, focusing on sensitive but widespread problems such as incest, teenage pregnancies, and venereal disease. Written in colloquial Jamaican English (locally referred to as the *patois* or 'Jamaica talk') by the station manager, this dramatic series was set in a village with a cast of characters with whom listeners could identify. The goal was to promote vicarious learning by listening to characters like themselves becoming aware of a problem, analyzing it, and then beginning to resolve it. The program was called *Pipeside* because it centered around the village water faucet where every villager stopped at some time or another—to flirt, fall in love, conceive illegitimate children, swap news, and fill water jugs. The community audience was invited to contribute script ideas, scripts, and their acting abilities. The characters and the dialogue were tested on the audience before final production to establish whether they were attention-getting, attention-holding, comprehensible, and useful.

Audience Involvement

The most significant part of audience involvement in program development was the local news. The challenge was to do an on-air simulation of the casual everyday exchange of news that takes place in church, in the rum bar, at the post office and at the bus stand. Three alternative formats were tested: straight reading of the news in broadcast-quality 'proper' English, a straight reading of the news in colloquial Jamaican English dialect, and a dramatic dialogue on news of the day between villagers speaking in the dialect. The audience chose the dramatized version of the news presented in their own dialect.

Radio was affirming their cultural identity and giving them a legitimacy on the air that had been reserved for British and American accents. In addition to this emotional value, there were cognitive gains too: the audience stated that they understood the radio news for the first time. Thus, the audience made the decision on how to treat local news. The next challenge was to collect news from and about the several hundred villages, so as to be able to share it. Government and nongovernmenttal agencies sent public relations news releases to the station, villagers did not. Therefore, the station ran several news collection and news production courses for all interested village receivers. High school teachers attended, as did students, illiterate farmers, and health workers. These news volunteers forwarded their news dispatches with travelers going to Mandeville, the central market town where the station was located. Many a country bus driver left his engine running and his passengers waiting outside Radio Central to drop off the news that a farmer had sent. Apart from being the farmer's favourite program, the local news program attracted the interest of press journalists from the capital city where it could not be heard. Their articles were favourable, but one did mention the contradiction between a government radio station that was celebrating the indigenous West African *patois* end of the Jamaican-English continuum, while the government school system was struggling to get children to speak at the anglicized end. The community radio station believed they should use the same idiom spoken in farmers' homes for effective communication since the home and farm was where they listened to radio.

The elite felt Jamaica should leave its West African past behind and prepare for greater integration into the language and lifestyles of such metropolitan centers as London and New York. This radio station's celebration of indigenous Jamaican culture became the subject of dinner table conversation in Kingston dining rooms oriented to New York and London. (This is not surprising since it was the Conservative Party in power that had insisted on all government officials wearing suits and ties during office hours.) In time, conversation moved on to other topics since the station was not heard in Kingston, but not before several chastising calls to the station from Cabinet ministers and their wives had led to a dilution of 'dialect' usage.

Even though villagers asked for programs to help solve their agricultural and health problems, their chief expectation of radio was entertainment. Hence, most of the programing was devoted to music, based on music preferences expressed by the community. Since the average farmer was

48 years old, his/her choice of music favored traditional Jamaican music like *mento*, 1950s gospel music, and country and western music. For the teenagers who were preparing to migrate to Kingston, the station played local Jamaican artists to provide them with role models to imitate from among local talent such as Bob and Rita Marley. By affirming national cultural strengths, the station hoped to develop a bulwark against the waves of American music that washed in from Miami, from their own national radio transmitters in the capital city, and from their tourist town of Montego Bay. A Jamaican music composer was hired to compose a signature tune that featured indigenous harmonies, rhythms, and instruments: the audience heard several versions on cassettes before they decided.

Thus, the USAID-financed rural community station of the Government of Jamaica's broadcasting system gave program development responsibility back to the people of Central Jamaica. The audience became the source: through their direct inputs and indirectly through an audience researcher hired to get audience input in the formative stages of program development (hence the name *formative* research). Through formative research, the community dictated what time the station should be on the air, what language they wanted their programs in, what topics they wanted information on, and what music they preferred.

Later Developments

But this glory was short-lived. The end of the USAID contract seemed to signal a return to 'business as usual' for the staff at the local station and the bosses at headquarters. The station manager now found she had to deal with additional bureaucratic requirements of accounting, administration, and constant authorizations that had been previously ignored by this experimental station. Within her own tiny staff, she found she had to battle unwilling producers who were fatigued by the extra workload and time required for program production with the audience as the decision maker. Their peers in other stations merely spun discs in air-conditioned studios, while they, the lower paid rural producers, had to face a daily routine of dust, heat, frequent rewrites, constant suppression of their own dramatic, linguistic and musical tastes, and a perpetual celebration of the villagers' preferences. Now that the USAID project agreement was over, headquarters staff and in-house staff showed little interest in continuing the intense audience consultations of the past. There was no foreign advisor checking on the process any longer. A year after the foreign aid contract was over, the station manager resigned because she could not cope with the frustration any longer.

Three years later, JBC's station in Central Jamaica was reduced to repeating the signal from the Kingston headquarters, for the most part. National advertisers had no complaints about JBC's transmission quality in Central Jamaica, thanks to the transmitter gifted to them by the citizens of the United States. JBC headquarters had fewer demands for gas and travel allowances from Central Jamaica since local staff rarely went to the village now. By all rights, USAID Washington should have been disappointed: the project did not generate any guidelines on how to use formative research as a strategic tool to run a community radio station. The village community that had enjoyed a few years in the control room was sorry they were evicted, but they had more important battles to fight: the daily struggle for food, clothing, and shelter continued. An unusual confluence of factors that had made it possible for the *audience* and the *source* to converge for a short period on an island one hour's flight from Miami was no more.

In September 1985, Jamaican Prime Minister Edward Seaga outlined his government's new media policy—'to move in the direction of profitability, what is now required', Mr. Seaga announced, 'is a divestment of the regional stations to the private sector... the lease will be set at levels predicated on the need to provide a commerical rate of return on the assets employed and will also be determined within the context of a more profitable operation designed to achieve and maintain financial viability.' The station is now a western classical music outlet called KLAS.

The Government of Jamaica's 1985 media policy and the actions of the Government of India's television monopoly in dismantling the rural Kheda transmitter both demonstrated a preference for profit-maximization over the needs of their rural majorities.

This case study has attempted to point to the complexity involved in designing mass media interventions that provide for the participation of national majorities. Communication planning, and predictions about successful adoption of innovative research methodologies at the micro-level are circumscribed by macro-level political actors and economic factors that are rarely considered in project design attempts. A community radio station in North East Jamaica financed by multilateral UNESCO aid and a community radio station in Central Jamaica financed through bilateral USAID are now leased to private parties for reasons of *profitability* by the Government of Jamaica.

At What Stages of Message Design is Audience Research Done?

Audience researchers are usually hired after a message has been disseminated to establish what proportion of its intended audience was exposed to it. This research is of little use to a media producer who wants suggestions from the audience at the formative stages of message design to increase his/her chances of mobilizing the community. An audience research-based message design system should schedule time, staff, and transport resources for audience research at two stages in the media production process—preproduction and midproduction. Preproduction audience research investigates what the intended audience knows and wants to know of the broad topic area assigned to the production team, e.g., child abuse. It also includes data collection on how the audience would prefer information on this topic presented to them for reflection, discussion, and action. Only after this data is collected by the researcher, should the producer, subject specialist, and researcher settle down to defining what media programs can hope to achieve on this topic (objectives) and what the content and form of the messages (specifications) should be. Midproduction, once rough versions of messages are ready, the audience researcher then collects data on audience reactions. At this stage, the message can still be revised to address problems in its attention-holding capacity, utility, or comprehension. The following case illustrates the results of lack of planning.

Lessons From Formative Research in the Satellite TV Experiment in India

In June 1967, a joint Indian Space Research Organization-National Aeronautics and Space Administration (ISRO-NASA) study found that a terrestrial-cum-satellite TV system would be the most cost-effective for India. ISRO proposed a one-year pilot project to provide insights on the configuration of such a TV system, its software, hardware, management, and cost aspects. This was the SITE project, the Satellite Instructional TV Experiment, conducted in 2,338 villages in India from August 1975 to July 1976, using a NASA satellite.

The two space agencies included the following 'instructional objectives' in the 'memorandum of understanding' they signed in September 1969. No attempts were made at further specification.

Primary Objectives:
– Contribute to family planning
– Improve agricultural practices
– Contribute to national integration
Secondary Objectives:
– Contribute to general school and adult education
– Contribute to teacher training
– Improve other occupational skills
– Improve health and hygiene

These should more appropriately be called 'broad instructional areas'. Not unlike many educational projects before SITE, this project too, had no precisely spelled out behavioral goals that specified what behavior the viewer ought to be able to perform, under what condition, and with what level of confidence.

The primary responsibility for message-making was with the specially set up TV Satellite Wing in All India Radio (AIR), in the Ministry of Information and Broadcasting. With only two years to the first day of transmission, this wing had a lone director, one typist, no budget and no staff, and a 1,300-odd hours transmission requirement for August 1975-July 1976. Contrast this with the one-new-transmitter-a-day pace when the goal was sports coverage and commercialization in 1987.

In July 1974, three studios came up. Until then, AIR had been a news, public affairs, and music organization with a limited and less prestigious program for farmers' forums. Its organizational structure was not designed for development-support programing, and the new Satellite TV Wing reflected this. To add to their problems, AIR had great difficulty in getting program specifications laid down by agriculture, health, family planning, education, and other ministries that its broadcasting was supposed to be supporting. Each of these departments had their problems too—they did not have financial sanction to appoint a full-time content expert or liaison for the SITE project. Someone was often named as a matter of form who already had 101 other jobs to do in his/her own ministry. How should AIR decide what to produce with overburdened or nonexistent content experts?

The systems analysts and the specially-recruited summative evaluators in the Indian space agency felt that empirical data on village conditions should determine the objectives and curriculum, rather than only the opinions of overworked experts in government secretariats far from the village. But whose job was it? Shouldn't each development agency that wanted broadcasting support do its own study of communication needs in the villages, define instructional goals, and specify a content plan for each program that the creative genius of the broadcasters could then flesh out? All that happened was a series of meetings at state and central government capitals where experts drew up a 'list of topics' for the programing organization. Television-user ministries did try to supply scripts as often as they could, even though they lacked scriptwriting skills, some ministries doing better than others. But coordinated scheduling of activities was always a problem in an interministerial undertaking where each agency had different priorities. The space agency had thought of a satellite, but the broadcasting agency and the development departments felt they had been doing adequately without it.

The summative evaluators in the space agency (located over 1,000 miles from the producers) with academic training in anthropology, sociology, psychology, and communications, had never heard of terms like 'formative evaluation'. They decided they would try to provide context and input evaluation data in addition to the impact evaluation they were hired to do, on which they were already behind schedule and understaffed.

Context evaluation provided profiles of life at the village level, and an assessment of needs in the SITE instructional areas.

Ethnographic data collection and secondary sources provided the basis of audience profiles. They presented non-technical, generalized pictures of dialects spoken, food habits, dress, religion and ritual, and a typical working day. The producers' reactions were that the reports were 'too simple'. This SITE researcher then wrote up a more technical fact-filled socioeconomic profile for the space agency's own producers on items for which they requested data on. It is doubtful that they ever read it. In the SITE Continuity phase, photographic albums were therefore prepared, which could also help in costuming, set designing, and characterization. One station director locked them up in his desk because he felt they were too beautiful to be used by all and sundry... but it was clear that the city-based TV producers who could not make visits to their rural target audiences greately preferred the visual form of presentation.

ISRO social researchers assessed needs by interviewing district, block, and village level officials in agriculture, health, and education, since there was no time to study the villagers' perceptions directly. An open-ended exploration conducted by this author in Rajasthan showed that there were big differences in the villagers' and officials' opinions, particularly regarding the causes of problems. Subsequent content analyses of SITE programing did not reflect utilization of the content of the reports. Of uneven quality, they too were first attempts like many other things in SITE. Apart from being written documents, they came when producers were busy canning programs—the time for planning content and formats was past. If they had come earlier, there would have been no producers on the staff to read them. Mainly fresh recruits, the producers went from topic-listing ministry meetings, to the studio floors. Either way, the needs assessments were a well-intentioned effort that did not have a chance.

Input evaluation was supposed to consist of prototype testing in the village. With each producer canning one feature-length production a month from the word 'Go', there were no prototypes to test. Whatever was made first was tested, and thus one of the two sessions proposed per state were completed. This was in the face of monstrous problems in obtaining portable VTRs for village playback, engineers' reluctance to let studio equipment face dust storms, heat, and the monsoon rains. One or two producers would accompany the research team: those who were interested in the rural development cause of the project were genuinely interested in whether their programs were working, those who were looking for praise for their artistic statements were appalled at the testing sessions, uncomfortable in the village, and generally obstructionist. The first two of the half-dozen testing sessions held were, in fact, explosive, because both species were testing each other out. The researcher was preoccupied with evolving a satisfactory methodology, given the logistics problems of transport, power failures in the middle of playback, and the like, rather than concentrating on the producer's sensitivities. The pretesting reports were requested in nontechnical terminology and carried general tips like the following:

> avoid starting an evening transmission with a lullaby—the viewers have come from a hard day of manual labor and

are. relaxing in front of the TV with the hubble-bubbles, and that's all they need to make them snore through the rest of your instructional programing; keep the soporific soothing rhythms for last; long-shots do not hold the viewers who are sitting 20 feet from the screen; restrict yourself to a new cinematic language that has only close mid-shots, mid-shots and mid-long shots; many viewers have never seen moving pictures before, so go easy on extreme close-ups and quick zoom-ins; the national interest will not serve as an impetus for any behavioral change when individual food, clothing, and shelter needs are not met; tell the viewer what he/she will get out of the change you are suggesting.

Clearly, many of the guidelines were commonsensical. Producers taunted researchers on whether their research could tell them anything that they did not know already. The researchers restrained themselves from pointing out that the test programs had contained these commonsensical errors, and hence the common sense tips suggested.

Researchers hoped that the findings from the audience profile and the needs assessment would help define precise goals, along with the expertise from the specialists. The pretesting was to help finalize persuasive appeals and forms. But SITE software had got organized too late.

The marvelous thing about SITE software was not its last-minute formative research attempts, or the fact that no time and money were allocated for formative research. The miracle is that there was a passable program ready to go on the air every day for four hours a day.

What Does Message Design Research Cost?

In grass roots organizations where the community worker is the media producer, it is perfectly appropriate for him/her to do his own rough-and-ready audience research as well. The crucial resource is *time*.

In large media production organizations located in urban areas at a distance from their audiences, the costs of doing anything are higher than in small community groups. Media producers, subject specialists, and audience researchers have distinct professional roles and salary requirements. The addition of audience research to the media production process implies the addition of salary and office space for a researcher, vehicle availability for audience visits at two time points, and the budgeting of time in the production schedule for these activities.

Who Will Do the Audience Research?

Many communication organizations prefer to have formative evaluators in-house, given that audience-based program development through formative evaluation involves preproduction needs assessments and media habits studies, preferably in collaboration with the producer, to define what the audience wants to know, and then midproduction feedback from the audience, again preferably in collaboration with the producer. They are either in a separate audience research department in the organization, or assigned to production teams working on particular series. The pioneering attempt in in-house team production is the facility set up by Edward Palmer, former Vice-President for research at the Children's Television Workshop (CTW) in New York. CTW produces several educational products in addition to the famous *Sesame Street*. Examples of other communication organizations with in-house formative evaluators include the rural television stations that are part of the Indian National Satellite system (INSAT), the Agency for Instructional Television in Bloomington, Indiana, the Open University in England which produces materials in all media for college education outside university walls, and the Ontario Educational Communication Authority in Toronto, Canada.

Manufacturers of new equipment send their prototypes to independent test and evaluation agencies to evaluate whether they meet their specifications. Using an independent unbiased outsider is an appropriate method of message pretesting too, when the team has clearly specified goals against which to measure the program. Third World governments which do substantial development communication work might want to set up an independent objective pretesting agency that benefits from the experiences of the US government's Health Message Testing Service.

An *audience-based* development communication team makes a commitment to be accountable to the community at the planning, implementation, and evaluation stages. An *ideal* team would require representation in three areas of expertise: the subject or development content, media production skills, and formative evaluation of messages. An audience researcher is responsible for systematically collecting and analyzing data regarding what the audience wants information on, a subject specialist is responsible for being up-to-date on the topic and how to communicate, and a writer-producer is responsible for developing a program that will communicate the needed information. These may be three separate people, but then again, they may not. One person may have expertise in two of the three areas. The budget of the grass roots organization may be able to afford only one person who will be expected to perform all three roles. Needless to say, the introduction of team responsibility leads to new problems—the problem of communication between members of the team who come from different disciplines, speak different languages, each person wanting total control over the process.

Table 4.1 shows the individual and joint responsibilities of the team for each of the steps in audience-based development communication message design. This listing does not reflect the heavy load on the writer-producer's shoulders in all media productions, irrespective of the intensity of audience dialogue before and during production. It lists only those steps that are unique to this audience-based mode of production. The formative evaluator is the primary liaison with the audience, and is therefore mentioned frequently. He/she has primary responsibility for *listening* to the audience to help determine topics and form. This implies conducting the audience's lifestyle and communication preferences analysis, assessing the needs, writing goals and message specifications, pretesting draft messages, and monitoring the process of message reception after distribution. The subject specialist is responsible for providing locally appropriate solutions to audience problems. While it is desirable that all three team members participate in all activities, the listing below specifies the *degree* of responsibility of each of the three members, per activity.

Table 4.1

Responsibilities of Team Members in Audience-Based Production Mode

Activity	Primary Responsibility	Secondary Responsibility
1. Learn everything possible about the topic of the campaign	Subject specialist	Writer-Producer Formative evaluator
2. Analyze lifestyle and communication preferences of audience(s)	Formative evaluator	Writer-Producer
3. Assess audience needs vis-a-vis the campaign topic	Formative evaluator	Subject specialist
4. Write specific measurable goals	Formative evaluator	Subject specialist Writer-Producer
5. Select media	Producer-Writer	Formative evaluator
6. Agree on creative-persuasive strategy	Production-Writer	Formative evaluator
7. Write program specifications	Formative evaluator	Writer-Producer Subject specialist
8. Pretest	Formative evaluator	Writer-Producer Subject specialist
9. Modify message and proceed with mass production	Producer-Writer	
10. Monitoring exposure	Formative evaluator	Subject specialist Writer-Producer

Team production will work only if the organization assigns collective responsibility for achieving communication to the group of three, and evaluates them collectively on the basis of impact evaluation results from the *audience*. The division of responsibilities according to specializations frequently causes professionals to do *their* individual jobs, and not worry about the next step that the next person has to take. Part of this is due to the narrow training each professional receives: the media professional rarely learns what good audience research can do to improve the chances of communication, while the audience researcher has no understanding of the production process, its time pressures, and artistic temperament. Part of this is also due to evaluation based on individual roles, rather than on the basis of audience needs and preferences.

So who is the boss? The audience community should make the decisions on content and form to guarantee communication. But who is ultimately responsible for completing the job in time—for efficiency in bureaucratic terms? If this activity is housed in a family planning agency, the subject specialist frequently initiates the total project and hence assumes responsibility for completing it on time, and achieving its goals. If the project is housed in a media production agency, it is the media producer who is in charge. In both cases, it is rarely the formative evaluator. The audience liaison is crucial to the success of the project but always seems to play a supporting role. This is a very difficult role to play when the audience-based mode of production is new to the implementing organization. Project managers will resist it, because it takes more time. Media producers who are not accustomed to having the audience represented at every step of the production process will be offended by audience input on characters, sets, and story lines when they contradict their personal artistic judgements. Community-conscious media workers have professional egos too. In time, they learn that the formative evaluator and his/her systematic audience data can be a refuge when there is a storm of criticism from bosses, bureaucrats, and bullies, and provide the necessary reassurance about being on the right track for grass roots workers.

In many production situations, there is no money to hire the services of an outside formative evaluation service or hire communication researchers to work in-house. The intention of this book is to show the writer-producer and production assistant how to do preproduction and midproduction audience research themselves, rather than have none at all. Although the creativity required for media production cannot be taught, audience research skills can. The implication is that the media producer can learn the basics of conducting bias-free audience research. In a grass roots organization close to the community it serves, this may be the best approach. In a large production organization with deadlines and competition between producers on how many hours of production they can take credit for, it is not realistic to expect the producer to do his/her own audience research as well. Note the long list of activities that get added to a production if it is to be based on audience dialogue before and during production. Designing needs assessment studies systematically, and objectively testing audience attention, comprehension, and utility levels of one's own programs *impartially*, in addition to artistically producing an attention-holding radio program requires time. Creative social researchers and subject specialists who have basic artistic ability that could be developed further should be identified and recruited for media production training. A team will function more effectively when its members have some appreciation of the complexities and stresses of each other's roles. Curricula of training programs should be expanded to include exposure to the stresses of media production for audience researchers and exposure to formative evaluation methods for media producers.

The next chapter describes the variety of methods that the production team can use to collect information from their audience.

ETHICS

The preceding section has discussed audience research-based media production. It has provided case studies of problems that constrain utilization of this process—problems of time, staff, transportation, and political will. It is appropriate to pause and evaluate the ethics of this method: is it right or wrong—under which conditions? Who will use it, and in whose interest?

As indicated in Chapter 1, national development planning and implementation is usually initiated by the state in top-down fashion. Questions of social engineering and social control are inherent in such individual and societal change attempts. The mass media are deployed to persuade audiences to participate in the state's plans for agriculture, health, and education. Implicit is the need to transfer knowledge, change attitudes, and modify behaviors in populations that are invisible and inaudible. But research shows it is not easy to achieve 'communication' through the mass media (see the articles by McGuire and Dervin in Rice and Atkin).[2] The sender-receiver separation problem in all mass communication is compounded in applications such as government development-support when the content that is being diffused by planners at the 'top' is not sensitive to the needs of those at the 'bottom'. Will the use of formative research make the Third World state more successful in *manipulating* audiences to do what they are initially disinclined to do and are not consulted on? Will formative research help social marketing agencies to assess the needs of audiences so they can then 'package' their products to *appear* as if they are sensitive to community needs?

Both the preceding scenarios are possible, since audience re-search-based message design is only a method. It is a strategic device that approximates the dialogue-based route to communication through interpersonal interaction. This is achieved by organizing sender/producer visits to the audience before and during production of messages to be delivered through one-way mass media.

Under what conditions is audience research-enhanced message design right or wrong? The production of any message involves selection of one set of content over another, and manipulation of symbols that represent meaning—words, gestures, characters, sets, costumes, music, etc. *Directive use of audience research* to help achieve someone else's goals is devious and wrong. When the state's goals are contrary to people's wishes, the situation is problematical. A common present-day illustration is the use of state media campaigns to persuade villagers to leave their ancestral homes against their will because the government wants to build a dam (that will flood their homes) to generate electricity for neighboring cities. Under conditions when the sender's interests and the audience's preferences are in opposition, message designers who have the benefit of such data must be skeptical, hesitant and critical of the power structure, and consistently respectful of human beings.

Preproduction audience research identifies community fears and insecurities in addition to community strengths that could be used by the message designer to achieve an assigned goal. Vindictive-ness, jingoism, racism, and xenophia are elements of human nature. Should the audience researcher urge that these base appeals be used as means to achieve the end, *because* they are bound to be effective? Such appeals predominate in government media campaigns at times of war and crisis. Truth is frequently sacrificed when media campaigns make some group or some country out to be the villainous cause of the national problem. National propagandists, media producers and researchers who choose to play on the negative elements of our humanity to reach their goals may win the immedi-ate battle but contribute to losing the long-time war all of us wage to better ourselves as a species, irrespective of the country we live in.

Under what conditions would the strategic use of audience research for effective communication be right? An ideal scenario would be a grass roots organization or a local government agency which wants to assess community needs and then use the media to present alternative problem-resolution possibilities for community reflection, leading to the evolution of a self-development and national transformation plan. Audience research would be involved in *nondirective*, open-ended needs assessment, and pretesting of messages featuring alternative problem-solving possibilities. As stated in Chapter 1: self-sustaining development requires educated consent and informed participation. The complementary communication process that flows from this conceptualization implies mobilization through accurate information provision for all, and not message design to elicit compliance to the wishes of some authority, no matter how well-intentioned it may be.

Inferences made from a superficial review of selected world religions indicate a range of opinions on the acceptability of directive audience research-based message design.[3] In the Hindu caste system, it is acceptable for members of the highest caste, the Brahmin priestly caste, to guide and control the lower castes. Under the Islamic code, *imam*-ordered manipulation of the public is acceptable only if it is a part of a *jihad* (struggle) for a better life for all. Because of its goal of removing ignorance and dissemination of truth to all, Buddhism comes down clearly in support of nondirective audience research for message design. In Judaism, the leaders are entrusted with the responsibility to guide their community; manipulation would be acceptable only within the community, and only as part of this trust. Because of its goal of actively maintaining harmony (*li*) in society, Confucianism would accept manipulation by those in higher positions of authority and responsibility. Taoism teaches that any interference with the 'way of nature' (*tao*) is wrong. Thus, any form of engineering—social or physical—is not acceptable. A general concept that cuts across many African traditional religions is belief in a hierarchy of power, based partly on age and partly on status within the tribe. The leader is allowed to manipulate the community in his wisdom. In Christianity,[4] both senders and receivers are regarded as being 'created in the image of God' and are required to love one another. To persuade fellow humans to behave differently from the way they do, and more like the way powerful client groups would want them to, would violate this ethic if this persuasion were not based on goodwill for others. *Agape* is the Christian ideal: unselfish, other-directed love. To reduce human beings to only instrumental value is unloving and thus wrong.

When the audience's interests and the sender's needs diverge, audience sensitivity is only a 'means' to achieve the sender's 'ends'. This is when formative evaluation deteriorates into collection of 'audience intelligence' information on what local words and gestures to use to persuade the audience to do what someone else wants— in their own interest or in what someone else perceives is in the audience's interest. These conditions violate ethics based on several religions, and the Kantian categorical imperative. For Kant, what is right for one is right for all, with no extenuating circumstances.

A part of the ethical guidelines of the National Association for Practicing Anthropology is instructive for development communication producers and researchers:[5]

> **Our primary responsibility is to respect and promote the welfare and human rights of all categories of people affected by decisions, programs or research in which we take part. It is our ethical responsibility to bring to bear on decision making, our own or that of others, information concerning the actual or potential impacts of such activities on all whom they might affect. It is also our responsibility to assure, to the extent possible, that the views of groups so affected are made clear and given full and serious consideration by decision makers and planners, in order to preserve options and choices for affected groups.**

The key to ethical decision making is caring about other people. An ethical production team would place a very high priority on how their conduct affects others. Does the disinterested nature of public service 'ends' in some development communication campaigns on agriculture, health, nutrition, and education make audience research-based manipulation of the audience acceptable? Utilitarians would hold that the ethically correct action is the one that produces the greatest good for the greatest number of people while inflicting the least harm on the fewest number. Therefore, a utilitarian might argue that media programs that teach audiences to grow more food meet the greatest good requirement; the harm of manipulation is minor in comparison with the actual danger of starvation. Others would point out that not all agriculturists agree on the ends pursued in an agriculture campaign: high-yielding variety crops for sale or traditional varieties for comsumption. There is no agreement on what the best interests of the public are. Thus, even development communication campaigns promote interests valued by *some* powerful group that may or may not be representative of the people. As such, the ethical distinctions between advertising and public sector campaigns are irrelevant. In fact, the profound nature of goals of many development communication campaigns generally have far greater implications for values and lifestyles than the decision to switch from one brand of toothpaste to another.

Persuasive communications are notorious for their reliance on 'treatment' over 'topic', style over substance. Invariably, they present part of the story (exaggerated promises, incomplete disclosures) and are, therefore, biased. The ethical question is: are the promises and expectations they raise accurate?

The media are 'means' to an end. For the commercial sponsor of a radio or television drama, the end is audience maximization. For the development agency, the end may be mobilizing the nation to reconsider oppressive roles assigned to their women. Frequently, the financier's goal dilutes the development agency's goal, when they conflict. If male audience members with purchasing power do not like questions that are raised about their treatment of women in a particular series, the program sponsor will request modification and dilution of the problematic theme. If a head of state does not like the prosocial theme, no matter how ethically it might be portrayed, he/she may order the show off the air. A grass roots agency which works with women may find dramatic portrayals of offensive behavior against women that their constituency would like to change has the opposite effect on men—it legitimizes and confirms the negative behaviors.

William J. Brown and Arvind Singhal[6] report how the traditional subservient mother in the Indian commercial soap opera *Hum Log* was chosen as a positive role model worth emulating—by women! They highlight four ethical dilemmas about 'prosocial' messages, that is, content that depicts activities supposed to be socially desirable by *most* members of an audience. They are: (*i*) how to distinguish prosocial from antisocial; (*ii*) how to ensure that all groups of people are portrayed with equality and dignity; (*iii*) how to respond to unintended consequences of prosocial messages; and (*iv*) basically, is it unethical to use media as a persuasive tool to guide social development.

Research has shown that some media programs have had powerful influences on some audiences at particular points in time, e.g., the 1938 Halloween broadcast of H.G. Wells' *War of the Worlds* frightened 1 million of its 6 million US viewers who thought it was news about a real invasion from Mars. In Lima, Peru, a local adaptation had a devastating aftermath: when the Peruvian audience discovered that a radio program had tricked them and that the world was not coming to an end, they burned the radio station to the ground.

Some individuals and groups have limited ability to discern what is true, appropriate, honest, fair, or just because of youth, limited education, low access to other sources of information, or highly suggestible personalities. Manufacturers and commercial sponsors of messages who operate in the private sector take refuge behind the adage, *Let the Buyer/Message Receiver Beware.* Is formative evaluation that is designed to increase a program's capability to communicate particularly problematic for such people? Is it unethical to use formative evaluation as a means when the end is, for example, to influence children to pester their parents to buy another new toy, or to persuade low-income slum dwellers who can hardly afford to buy milk for their children once a week to spend their scarce purchasing power on the new local soft drink that the national government is producing?

The laws of most nations give individuals the right to free speech and the right to receive information. To dialogue with potential audiences in the hope of designing communications that will influence their attitudes and change their behaviors is not illegal, on the one hand. But is it ethical to use this freedom to introduce high-yielding varieties of grain from foreign labs that will change traditional cultural ways of growing food? While more food will help improve dwindling food supply that threatens the existence of the community, will it irrevocably change local ways of adapting to natural environments from which this audience community drew its coherence and moorings? On the other hand, is it condescending and maternalistic for this author to assume that audience communities consisting of individuals with free wills cannot discriminate between ends for themselves? Or that they will not be able to discern content that is economically, politically, or spiritually repugnant to them because of its clever creative-persuasive packaging? We know that historical conditions of underdevelopment and poverty have affected individuals and groups in countries of the South differentially. A few advanced, the many did not. Education to critically evaluate information from sources in power is unevenly distributed. Given the environment of mass media messages we live in, it is necessary that consumers be educated to critically decipher the information content they are surrounded by, irrespective of its source.[7] Formative evaluation for communication design is generally deployed by the two central power players in society today, the state and market forces. The degree to which message receivers can exercise their critical judgement and free will is limited by options permitted and promoted by the state and market forces.

In light of the preceding questions, it is clear that a development communication production team needs to exercise caution on goals, treatment, and consequences, intended and unintended, short-term and long-term. When grass roots organizations use formative evaluation to reduce misunderstanding in their horizontal communications with each other, the audience is source and receiver, means and end. This is the participatory ideal, what Habermas[8] calls the *ideal speech situation*. When the goal is not the people's own, formative evaluation uses audience research as a means to an end. While most audiences may actively and maturely process information to protect their own interests, it is conceivable that some messages packaged creatively in the local idiom will receive less scrutiny than they deserve by some vulnerable populations. Clearly, then, every member of a production team must take responsibility for the ethics of the goal it is promoting in a particular context, irrespective of whether he/she is the subject specialist or the media producer or the formative evaluator. This means satisfying oneself to the best of one's ability about the accuracy, truthfulness, and consequences of the knowledge, attitudes, and behaviors one is an accomplice in promoting.

Many foreign aid agencies (e.g., the UN's Food and Agriculture Organization, the US government's Agency for International

Development, and the private Rockefeller Foundation) promoted chemical fertilizers through agriculture extension media campaigns. The unforeseen consequences of soil depletion have resulted in new media campaigns, today exhorting farmers to go back to their traditional use of organic fertilizers! A frequently mentioned communication goal that had foreseeable consequences in economically constrained Third World living conditions is the successful promotion of bottle-feeding of infant formula to mothers who can breast-feed their newborns quite adequately. Unfortunately, a large proportion of mothers who started their infants on bottle-feeding did not have access to running water and fuel to sterilize the bottles. Because they were poor, they diluted the packaged formula to make it last longer, so the baby was actually receiving little more than colored water. Infant formula manufacturers such as Nestlé, American Home Products, Bristol-Meyers, and their domestic imitators in Third World settings, have used media campaigns and salespersons dressed as nurses in delivery wards, to distribute free introductory containers of their product. This has led to infant diarrhea deaths and changes in a locally appropriate, economical, and hygienically sound cultural system. A similar example is the marketing of pesticides. Marketing and product packaging that was not tailored to Third World country environments resulted in half of the world's pesticide poisoning cases and three-fourths of the world's pesticide deaths in regions that accounted for only 15 percent of world pesticide use. Promotional campaigns could not counteract the illiteracy, lack of training in pesticide handling, and inadequate safe space for storage far from food that contributed to the misuse of the product.

Finally, the role of the mass media, fine-tuned through formative evaluation, is often overemphasized and inappropriately suggested as a solution to a range of development problems. The roots of these problems are in the economic structure of society— who owns land, who can afford medical care—and are not amenable to public education alone. Is it ethical to spend limited national resources on expensive mass media campaigns in Third World settings that focus on symptoms rather than the cause, that address individuals rather than the structures of inequality and differential access to opportunities? What are the ethics of such potentially diversionary cosmetic attempts that provide an illusion of action but do not affect the prevailing order of priority and privilege? The mass media, carriers of public information campaigns, are invariably centrally controlled by the state and/or large private corporations. Messages financed by them will support their interests. One cannot expect the powerful state-private sector edifice to countenance media programs that question existing political and economic arrangements or the consumption ethic. The hope for development communication lies in grass roots groups and communities organizing a parallel system to meet their own information needs, making full use of lower-priced communication hardware and these message design research guidelines on how to *share meaning* successfully among their own membership, where sender and receiver are one.

Notes and References

1.   This is adapted with the publisher's permission from Bella Mody, 'The Receiver as Sender: Formative Evaluation in Jamaican Radio'. *Gazette*, 38, 1986, pp. 147–60.

2.   Ronald Rice and Charles Atkin, eds. *Public Communication Campaigns*. Newbury Park: Sage, 1989.

3.   Ritin Singh, graduate student in the Communication-Urban Studies program at Michigan State University, conducted the literature search and interviews with religious leaders that provides the basis of this section. Professor Alford T. Welch, of the Religious Studies Department at Michigan State University, very kindly reviewed this section.

4.   Professor Paul Soukop S.J. of Santa Clara University contributed this perspective.

5.   Jean Gilbert. 'Ethical Guidelines for Practicing Anthropologists'. *Anthropology Newsletter*, December 1987.

6.   William J. Brown and Arvind Singhal. 'Ethical Dilemmas of Prosocial Television'. *Communication Quarterly*, 38, 3, Summer 1990, pp. 268–80.

7.   Jeffrey Schrank. *Deception Detection*. Boston: Beacon Press, 1975.

8.   Jurgen Habermas. *Knowledge and Human Interests*. Boston: Beacon Press, 1971.

DESIGNING MESSAGES THAT COMMUNICATE 5

If anything can go wrong, it will, Murphy predicted. Osmo Wiio, the Finnish researcher, was half joking too when he wrote his cynical 'laws' of communication:[1]

1.   Communication usually fails; it succeeds only by chance.

1.1   If there is any way a communication can fail, it will.

1.2   If there appears to be no way a communication can fail, be sure it still will.

1.3   If communication seems to be have been successfully achieved, it must have happened in a way that was unintentional.

1.4   When you are certain your communication is bound to succeed, it is bound to fail.

2.   If a message can be understood in different ways, it will be understood in just the way that does the most harm.

3.   Somebody else always knows what you actually meant to communicate, better than you do.

4.   The more communication there is, the more difficult it is for communication to succeed.

4.1   The more communication there is, the more misunderstanding will occur.

5.   In mass communication, appearances are more important than the reality of how things actually are.

6.   The importance of a particular topic or issue depends on how closely it affects the life of the sender. It is inversely related to the square of the distance.

Most laws are hard to follow. Wiio's 'laws' are unusual, however: these cynical laws are hard to break without *special effort*. This book, then, is a compendium of systematic special efforts for those who want to achieve communication.

The first chapter reviewed what we know about mass media use for national development. This chapter reviews research on the effects of mass media, to identify lessons (if any) for national transformational applications. Admittedly, present applications are top-down while our transformational task needs bottom-up and horizontal communication to share meaning within groups and achieve solidarity across groups. The chapters that follow focus on the theory and application of the audience participation-based approach to message design.

Think of all the conversations you participated in today. Do you feel confident that the person(s) you were speaking with actually grasped the full meaning of what you tried to convey? After you finish making a major point with someone, or after giving a lecture, ask your listeners to list the main points you made. Teachers are accustomed to finding that their students can recall less than half the points in a lecture. You may be startled by what you find.

Information is frequently 'lost' in face-to-face presentation. Communicators who are forced to use technological media to bridge the distance between the sender and the receiver often find that communication failures are even worse than in face-to-face presentations. They discover that the packaging (the 'message') was delivered but not the contents (the 'meaning'). The intended meaning was distorted or lost in transit due to economic, political, and sociocultural inappropriateness, audience filters and the physical barriers of distance. *Information loss* occurs when the audience does not receive part or all of the intended meaning. *Information distortion* occurs when the meaning received by the audience is a modified form of the meaning that the production team intended to share.

'Mass' Communication—Is it Possible?

Theories and practitioners' suggestions, notwithstanding, it is very difficult to 'communicate' (that is, achieve an identity of meaning between sender and receiver) with 'masses' of people without first dialoguing about the problems on their minds and their different ways of knowing. If it were possible to stop using the term 'mass communication', we might all be better off. It refers to the design of information products in media factories (i.e., studios) by professionals, and the distribution of these products through technological devices (radio, television, satellites) to individuals and families scattered over a wide area. It cannot mean actually achieving an identity of meaning between a sender and a massive number of receivers because that is rare. Unfortunately, use of the term is frequent, and frequently carries the latter meaning. The term 'mass communication' arose from the sociological concept of 'mass society'. Sociologists feared that close human ties to families, friends, traditions, and work typical of the former agricultural society had been severed by the emergence in the West of an urban industrial society. They feared that people would not have close personal connections in this new form of society. Information channels would have great power to control, and manipulate this 'lonely crowd' of isolated individuals. The media of this 'mass society' were therefore called the *mass media*. The term began to appear in the English language in the 1940s to describe radio, movies, and newspapers.

Sociological researchers in North America and Western Europe later found that the need to work in assembly lines and to live in cities had indeed created anonymity, but that personal ties, though weakened, had not disappeared. Communication research did not find the media of the new industrial society to be as powerful as advertisers had hoped and as mass theorists had feared. Research on the effects of the mass media conducted in the United States from the late 1940s was reassuring in terms of the society's well-being: far from being passive and easily manipulable, audiences selected which media and which messages they would attend to and which they would allow to influence them.[2] Most people made such decisions after talking to their families, their friends, and the experts they trusted; audiences did not blindly do what the media told them to do.[3] Audience response depended on the source of the information, the emotional appeals built into the message, the structure of the message, and the nature and initial attitudes of the audience. Several large-scale surveys found that media campaigns had limited or no effect on the public's voting decisions and knowledge of public affairs. Experiments conducted by the US Army on the use of films to persuade soldiers reported similar findings.[4] A massive advertising budget may get people to switch from one brand to another. It can cause audiences *predisposed* to labor-saving devices to try a new product, but it does not change our basic preferences.

Currently, the limited effects model seems to have been abandoned in the United States for a powerful effects model—under limited source, message, channel, and receiver conditions. This model conceives that a communication could have 100 percent impact on a specified 10 percent of the population. What caused this switch?

The dominance of television in the daily schedules of US homes has increased steadily since the 1960s. The programing is increasingly saturated with violence. With simultaneously rising crime rates, assassinations, and riots, researchers are again looking for evidence that television has powerful effects. The 1971 US Surgeon General's Report (unfortunately dominated by industry-approved communication researchers) stated that it was difficult to distinguish the influence of one medium from a complex array of societal forces.

In 1982, the US National Institute of Mental Health summarized ten years of subsequent research. They reported that *some normal youngsters did become more aggressive as a result of heavy exposure to televised violence*. Albert Bandura's elaboration of social learning theory[5] showed that behaviors portrayed in the mass media could be a source of learning about how to behave. These portrayed behaviors could become a more or less permanent part of the person's mode of coping with recurring problems. Researchers saw an increasing use of television in election compaigns. They questioned whether campaign designers could be spending millions on television unless they had strong reasons for believing it to be effective.

Some feel that the cyclical changes in the perception of media power among US researchers are not supported by actual research findings. Research procedures modeled on the *physical* sciences are not sensitive to the subtle, indirect, cumulative impacts of such ubiquitous *social* forces as television. McGuire[6] concluded that documented media impacts are so small as to raise questions regarding about their practical significance and cost-effectiveness, and that *special efforts* are required if the multiplicative potential of the media is to be harnessed. The systematic audience dialogue-based approach outlined in Chapter 3 is a *special effort* based on this recommendation.

All mass media messages are products of particular national economic, political, cultural, and geographical forces. Thus, one can expect the effects of media messages in different countries to be specific to their particular production environments that determine what can be said, and how. As the politics and economic situations of societies change, their media uses change as well, and their effects on each other. Thus, generalizations about '*media*' effects from the United States of America, or Japanese findings must be tested in other contexts before they are used in decision making in Kenya, Nigeria, or Pakistan. Since the largest amount of research on media effects has been done in the United States, we review (circumspectly) what most US media effects researchers generally hold to be true in our quest for insights on transformational applications of the mass media in distinct Third World settings.

Adults and children can and do learn from all media. Media influence usually takes place through changing what we know (cognitions). Cognitions, in turn, influence attitudes and behaviors. Audience members of higher socioeconomic status acquire information from the media at a faster rate than audience members of lower socio-economic status. Thus, the knowledge gap between the two groups increases, unless special measures are taken to prevent this from happening.

The media can provide knowledge about people and places that audiences cannot see or visit. The media can explain abstract principles by illustrating them in visual, concrete terms. Some media are better able to do this than others. The media can give prestige and status to people they feature. The media can focus attention on issues that audiences should think about—the media set the agenda. How audiences interpret media messages and what actions they take depends on them. The effects of messages are the *audience's* knowledge and attitudes.

The media can be a powerful factor in the development of attitudes and behaviors on topics where little is known and no strong attitudes or behavior patterns exist. However, changing existing attitudes for national transformation is more difficult. Modeling theory, adapted from Bandura's social learning theory, is useful in such situations. To change a particular kind of behavior (e.g., landlords beating their labor, or wife beating), a media organization following Bandura's theory would frequently 'model' (portray) a preferred *alternative* (e.g., dialogue) for coping with stressful situations. The intended audience segment must perceive these presentations as locally viable, beneficial ways to deal with the situations that previously led to the behavior that is to be changed. If the individual sees the preferred behavior 'modeled' in media messages on many occasions, the assumption is that the individual will imitate the alternative behavior in a *relevant* personal situation. *If* the modeled behavior proves useful in coping with the situation, the individual will feel rewarded for trying this new alternative and will repeat it. Further exposure to media portrayals of the same alternative are needed to remind the individual (beaters) to use the same behavior again. With repeated use, the new behavior becomes the person's habitual way of handling that type of situation, unless it ceases to be effective and rewarding. The theory does not promise media producers that viewers will immediately and uniformly imitate all the prosocial behaviors they present on television and in films. Whether imitation may come later, with the new behavior slowly becoming a part of the audience's repertoire, will depend upon the appropriateness of the alternatives that the production team suggests, the frequency with which they are presented, and the number of times the audience tries them and finds them useful.

It is the groups we belong to and the people we respect who directly influence our attitudes. Characteristics of our societies facilitate or impede change: Media channels are only one aspect of society. Thus, media messages can question existing social norms, but, *alone*, they are not adequate for effecting meaningful group and societal transformation. However, *the media are effective as part of a larger social or political change effort involving many forces*, as in the fall of Marcos in the Philippines and 'Baby Doc' Duvalier in Haiti.

Even acting alone, like the constant drip from a faucet that stains the wash basin over time, consistent media portrayals on selected themes *can affect the* ideology, values, and worldview of media audiences *in the long run*. The constant orchestrated use of words, images, and themes in print and electronic media do shape the way people come to view their world. Logically, the mass media have become agents of socialization into the prevailing dominant economic, political, and cultural power structure. 'Big' technology-intensive media are expensive and are hence owned and controlled by the economic power structure to serve their own cultural and political interests. Commercials promote the notion of consumption as a means to status and happiness, not contemplation, asceticism, or pioneering do-it-yourself efforts. State-controlled news excludes alternative facts and perspectives, and thus cultivates support for the ruling party under the guise of national loyalty and patriotism. George Gerbner and his colleagues on the Cultural Indicators project in the Annenberg School of Communication at the University of Pennsylvania asserted that television had become the central cultural arm of US society—the more an audience views television, the more its view of social reality will reflect televised portrayals. Thus, definitions of reality and social norms are now transmitted by the mass media too. For example, there is consistent evidence that children and adolescents who view televised portrayals of violence obtain higher scores on several indicators of aggression than those who do not. Those who view violent television programing demonstrate more delinquency, fighting, and parent-child conflict.[7] Thus, constant exposure to a particular kind of media content can create an environment supportive of the values it epitomizes, be it supportive of media controllers' personal values, the law-and-order maintenance values of state-controlled media, or the materialistic values associated with advertiser-financed media.

Conceptualization of audience members as *active* participants in the communication process who are different from each other has resulted in *reception* analysis: research on how audiences construct *meanings* out of media offerings. Some subcultures, communities and groups across geographically dispersed areas produce meaning out of messages they receive in similar ways, as a result of their similar social, cultural, and political circumstances.[8] Identification of 'interpretive communities' which make common interpretations of a text facilitate achieving communication with massive far-flung audiences.

Selection of media to reach particular audiences can benefit from ethnographic research[9] on how patterns of media consumption are organized in everyday life. Watching television in a public place has a different significance for men and women, large landlords, and landless labor.

Audiences are not passive internalizers of media messages. Whatever the media presents is modified by the prevailing cultures of class, race, and gender. Partial acceptance, reinterpretation, and sometimes outright rejection of the *planned meanings* (and unplanned meanings) of messages are more likely. Effects of media messages need to be seen in a more complex manner than simple reproduction.

COMMUNICATION INPUTS AND AUDIENCE RESPONSES

What is the process of communication via the mass media? McGuire[10] summarizes the literature for researchers, with directions for further reading. His elaboration on the work of his predecessors at the Yale Psychology Department (Hovland, Janis, and Kelley[11]) is the intellectual base of most behavioral science theory on persuasive communication. It visualizes the process in terms of 'inputs' (messages) from the media production team, and audience responses or 'outputs' to be triggered by these messages.

Communication Inputs

The media producer's input decisions include who will appear to be the 'source' of the information (e.g., the president of the country, a physician, a happy farmer), what to say (and how much), through which media it will be said, to whom it will be addressed, and what will be the intended effect. Each of these factors may cause the loss or distortion of the meaning that the production crew hopes to share with the community.

Production Team-Related Factors

A. The production team's knowledge of and attitude towards particular topics (e.g., exploitation of agricultural labor) and audiences (e.g., agricultural labor) affects the quality of the production effort. A producer, subject specialist or audience researcher who comes from the same background as the audience may be more knowledgeable about their problems, but may share their caste and class prejudices that have enabled them to rationalize and accept their exploitation over generations. A producer, researcher or subject specialist from a different background may have a lot of learning to do about the audience, but may potentially be more objective in the process. Irrespective of their place of birth, some feel it is below their dignity to design materials for poor audiences. Many 'subject specialists' (in agriculture or health, for example) may be up-to-date with scholarly journal articles but are out of touch with what is happening in their content area at the *grass roots* level of the community. Many researchers often display a patronizing attitude toward media audiences.

   Careful selection and training of staff can overcome part of this problem. How the winner of the first UNESCO Rural Communication prize did it is instructive. The predecessor of the Development Education Communication Unit (DECU) at the Space Applications Center in Ahmedabad, India, let it be known that their goal was 'Television for the Oppressed'. They hired only those creative producers and researchers who were committed to rural transformation. The leadership, organizational mission, and the minimal bureaucracy they then offered were partly responsible for their success. DECU's predecessor also invited subject specialists who worked at the grass roots level (Kheda in Gujarat) and knew community needs from their daily interactions to join their production teams. Preproduction audience dialogue on their needs (needs assessment studies) determined what the receivers knew, felt, and did. This, in turn, determined the topics for programing. The format of presentations evolved through midproduction audience dialogue for testing of titles, concepts, characters, sets, story lines, and tryouts of 'roughs' (described in Chapter 10).

B. Media production skills differ between individual producers, just as skills differ within the medical profession or the teaching profession. Media consumption habits (e.g., reading, viewing television) differ significantly between producers and their audiences, as well. When time and transport are built into the production budget for preproduction and midproduction dialogue with the audience, to fine-tune the topic and treatment of the program, the challenge of communicating with audiences with distinct media habits becomes less formidable. Given the differences between producers and audiences of unlike backgrounds, it is crucial to study the audience's information processing behaviors *before* designing a communication for them.

C. The position of the producer in the hierarchy of the media organization frequently determines the level of organizational resources and support she/he can command to make her/his program effective. Senior producers and artists may find it easier to get access to good audience researchers, transport for fieldwork and large budgets sanctioned than junior staff. The audience-based approach levels all such differences: big budgets and 'big' media do not guarantee the achievement of communication. The extent to which the content and the form of the message fits audience needs and preferences makes the difference.

D. The effectiveness of a message also depends on characteristics of the 'sender' perceived by the audience, e.g., the film star, the successful farmer, or the religious leader who actually delivers the message. Identifying a source that is perceived as an expert and trustworthy for different audience groups should be determined through audience dialogue rather than be based on the producer's best guess. Preproduction audience data collection helps remove the need for such 'guesstimates'.

Content-Related Factors

A. The economic, political, and cultural power structure: issues are often addressed in the public media in response to the activities of business leaders, political leaders, and religious-tribal heads. Media content is packaged/presented by city-based governmental media agencies far removed from life in the rural areas. No matter how good the 'production values' of the presentation, the content will be of little interest to the audience to whom it is disseminated, unless it is based on an assessment of their needs, a study of their information consumption habits, and systematic pretests of 'roughs', as illustrated in Chapter 10.

B. How to present controversial issues about national transformation such as redistribution of land, or abolition of race and caste discrimination? Should a message present one side or both sides of an argument? If opposing views are presented, will the first or the last one presented be more influential? Should the media message explicitly state a conclusion, or should the audience be left to discuss and draw their own? When are factual presentations better, and when are emotional ones superior? Midproduction audience dialogue (pretesting) (see Chapter 10) should determine the selection of format, treatment, and persuasive appeals.

Media-Related Factors

A. The physical availability of the material to the community: often, radio and TV signals do not cover all parts of a country with appropriate signal quality, if they reach them at all. Posters are frequently disfigured and stolen or displayed too high for the eye to see (to protect them from playful children). Clearly, it is crucial that the audience's lifestyle and media habits determine which delivery system and media mix are used to carry the message to its intended audiences.

B. Variations in sensory modalities (audio, visual), previous exposure to the channel, and the perceived credibility of each medium lead to differences in information exposure and retention. Differences in purchasing power, work habits, and the appropriateness of the viewing situation for all sexes, tribes, castes, and classes often result in individual and group differences in effects of different messages. One can expect low-income, less educated persons of the female sex to have low opportunity for exposure to the media in many settings. If communication is to be achieved, we must go beyond media planning that is based strictly on the numbers of people reached. The audience dialogue-based approach uses audience segmentation, specifying measurable goals for each audience segment. A media plan is tailored to each group, with content and format to match.

Audience-Related Factors

A. Limited knowledge of the language of the medium: an inability to understand the techniques that graphic artists, radio producers, and television producers use can lead to lack of communication. Many media producers forget to adapt the language of their medium (e.g., flashbacks and flash-forwards) to audiences who may have never seen moving pictures before. The most frequently repeated illustration is from Leonard Doob's work in Africa: audiences who had never seen enlarged photographs on a cinema screen dismissed the magnified malaria-carrying anopheles mosquito as something they did not need to worry about, because they did not have such large mosquitoes in their communities. Many filmmakers have experienced similar problems. George McBean and his colleagues in UNICEF have been trying to develop illustrations for print materials that will communicate with villagers who have low visual literacy.[12] Producers who aspire to be 'communicators' must tailor their products to the communication skills and habits of their audiences.

B. Attitudes toward the medium: differences in attitude toward the medium may lead to differences in individual exposure, comprehension, and retention of the message. Many parents feel television can adversely affect the reading and intellectual abilities of their children. Many people have strong attitudes about the ownership and control of the media. Some treat media financed by the state with skepticism because they believe it will present the 'sanitized' official version of news and public affairs. For others, media financed by advertising revenues is bad, because it is based on the lowest common denominator—the size of the audience that programs can attract. Advertiser-supported programing has a natural bias towards audience-maximizing program topics and audience-maximizing treatment of all topics. The audience dialogue-based approach to development communication can provide the data to determine which combination of media should be used to reach which audience segment, given their distinct preferences.

C. Differing knowledge about the subject: in addition to individual differences of opinion due to personality differences, audience segments come to the media with different life experiences. Differences in schooling and experiences acquired as members of a variety of political, religious, regional, and economic class groupings can lead to negative attitudes towards certain practices (e.g., cow slaughter or the eating of pork), beliefs (e.g., fire worship), and groups (e.g., particular occupations). What may make sense for the nation as a whole (e.g., family planning) may not make sense for individuals and communities (e.g., where more than half the infants die before 5 years of age). Successful persuasion takes into account the underlying reasons for attitudes, as well as the attitudes themselves. The audience dialogue-based approach shows media programs advocating specific transformations to *practices* build multiple contact points into

messages to cater to distinct multiple segments that
constitute the audience.

D. The social and economic status of the media receiver:
the ability of an individual to achieve a goal (set by the
community or by outsiders) is influenced by whether he/
she was born into a landless family in Bangladesh, a
majority tribe in Kenya, an untouchable caste in India,
or a religious group with very few members in Iran. A
person's socioeconomic status will affect his/her perception of the relative utility of media messages. Through
preproduction sender-receiver dialogue, it is possible to
tailor media messages to the socioeconomic backgrounds
of the audience.

E. The gender of the audience: present-day conceptions of
knowledge and truth have been shaped throughout history
(with a few exceptions) by the male-dominated majority
culture. It is now accepted that women's educational
needs and preferred styles of learning, knowing, and
valuing are different from men's. Men and women producers educated in male-dominated curricula focus on
male attributes of autonomy and abstract critical thought
and ignore the strengths of women's attributes such as
interdependence, intimacy, nurturance, and contextual
thought. Many more women than men define themselves
in terms of their relationships, connections, and responsibilities; men define themselves in terms of separation,
autonomy, and hence, their rights. Audience dialogue-
based message design must be sure to include the
woman's voice.[13] The potential for bias on the part of all
message designers selecting male samples for audience
dialogue is high. Like scientists, production teams could
make the mistake of generalizing what they have learned
from the study of men to the lives of women.

Context/Environment-Related Factors

A. The multiple stakeholders, influentials, and leaders who
condition the impact of the communication on the ultimate audience: messages in favor of agriculture and
small industry benefit many, but they can adversely affect

those who have had a monopoly on such information in the past. Many campaigns require the support of political leadership, economic powers, and cultural authorities (e.g., religious groups), if they are to make an impact in the short run and sustain their influence in the long run. UNICEF has done pioneering work on including mobilization of contextual forces into project design to increase the potential effectiveness of their media campaigns.

Neglect of producer, content, media, audience, and contextual factors can lead to communication materials that fail to communicate, i.e., posters, radio programs, television dramas, or films, where the format/treatment is inappropriate to the culture of the audience community and where the topic of the program is irrelevant to their problems, lifestyles, values, and needs. In the interpersonal communication process, the sender and listener can see each other and modify their positions, statements, style, and presentation, in response to information presented by the other. In designing a media product, the producer has to plan for all possible distorting factors, all handicaps and contingencies well in advance. There is no universal guideline as to how each of these inputs affects the output. The particular audience/topic/situation dictates the best combination in each case. Clearly, message design for effective communication seems to call for an audience dialogue-based perspective on sight, sound, and motion inputs.

Audience Responses

If messages are being designed for the sake of communication, then achieving identity of meaning between sender and receiver is the goal. Attention, interest, and perfect comprehension are the desired responses to a message. When messages are designed to support national transformation in behaviors and attitudes, then the desired sequence of audience outputs becomes longer and more complicated. A sequence of twelve outputs from the audience are desired: exposure to the message, attention, interest, comprehension, skills learning (if intended), attitude change (if intended), memorization for future use, recall through information search and retrieval (when memorized material is needed), decision making on the basis of retrieval, behavior in accordance with new meanings learned, reinforcement of behavior, and, finally, consolidation of the transformed position.

This input-ouput model assumes that if any of these steps do not occur, the goal of the communication campaign has not been met. It indicates that changes in any input can affect all the output steps, in different ways. Thus, every input (e.g., music, humor) aimed at improving some output (e.g., interest), must be tested in the early stages to ensure that it has the intended impact and that it does not have an unintended negative effect (e.g., distraction) at another stage (e.g., comprehension). While Chapter 10 describes how to conduct audience dialogue to pretest draft messages for exposure, attention, interest, comprehension, and potential for eliciting the transformation that is the campaign goal, it is harder to predict what effect some input will have on memorization or retrieval potential.

McGuire points out that if there were only a 50/50 chance for each step to occur, then the chance that transformed behavior (step ten) would take place is only 0.50 raised to the tenth power. This cold calculation is a very humbling datum to bear in mind when revolutionary regimes (e.g., Cuba, Nicaragua) and donor agencies such as USAID, UNESCO, or conventional national governments expect communication programs to play a major role in solving significant problems of national disintegration, AIDS transmission, or hunger.

Is this hypothetical twelve-step sequence the way all receivers process transformation-focused information? Our common sense and our research tell us the situation is even more complex. Audience response depends on a number of factors, such as what information is provided, as opposed to what the audience wants to know (e.g., smokers know why they should quit but need suggestions as to how they can successfully do so). The level of audience involvement with the issue (e.g., choosing between toilet soaps versus choosing between religions) will also affect how many steps in the sequence a receiver will take. Sometimes, audiences may have been forced to perform a certain behavior as part of a larger campaign (e.g., compulsory sterilization in a national family planning campaign for parents with more than a certain number of children) which resulted in behavior change before comprehension.

What should a media production team do? Michael Ray[14] has outlined two alternative sequences, depending upon the audiences's preexisting knowledge, attitudes, and behaviors. The **KNOW-FEEL-DO** hierarchy is the one popularized by McGuire. It is appropriate when the change that is being advocated is a major change for the audience (e.g., giving up traditional methods of cleaning one's mouth and teeth for a toothbrush and toothpaste). When the issue does not significantly involve the audience (e.g., choosing between brands of toothbrushes), it is probably a waste of campaign time to do much more than make the audience knowledgeable about the product prior to making it widely and easily available. Rather than designing messages about how much better potential users will feel if they try this new product or service, the recommended sequence would be **KNOW-DO (try)-FEEL**, in the hope that one trial will lead to positive feelings. The **DO-FEEL-KNOW** sequence addresses the alternative view of transformation that change in attitude is the consequence rather than the cause of behavioral change. Some believe that forced overt compliance will result in internal attitude change, and that without the force (e.g., violence, civil disobedience, legislation, the use of police), some strongly held attitudes (e.g., racial and religious-caste segregation in schools and residential areas) will not change.

Chapters 7 and 8 deal with how to determine the current knowledge, attitudes, and behavior of the intended audience so as to decide which hierarchy the communication team will use. When the topic of the message is very relevant to the audience, then motivation and ability to scrutinize issue-relevant arguments are high, and attitude changes that result are expected to last longer, to have greater chances of leading to behavioral change, and to demonstrate a strong resistance to counterpersuasion, according to Petty and Cacioppo.[15] In such a situation, treatment and format of presentation are peripheral and less important determinants of persuasion. The content carries the day, not the form. But, in many cases, when audience motivation and/or ability to process the arguments on a particular topic is low, the treatment or presentation format becomes central in getting and holding attention and, ultimately, in determining whether attitudes will change and how long such change will last. In such cases, it is not what is said but how it is said that will determine whether comprehension, attitude change, and behavior change take place. In some cases, then, there are fewer steps, as when the issue is a low-involvement one. And, in some cases, the steps take place in reverse order.

Other theories describe some of the motivational aspects of human nature that affect how different individuals process information. Such theories range from balance theory and dissonance theory that focus on achieving an equilibrium in terms of our thoughts (cognitions, what we know), to theories that focus on knowing more, i.e., cognitive growth theories. There are also 'feeling' theories, of which some focus on maintaining or reducing emotional levels, while others stress needs for emotional growth.

What should a message designer in Asia or Africa do with all this advice? What is the relevance of information processing theories of persuasion underlying Western public communication campaigns to societies where unemployment and underemployment are frequently over 50 percent, and individual freedoms exist merely on paper? Problems of underdevelopment have deep historical roots; they are complexes of economic, political, cultural, and technological elements. These are not the contemporary problems of North America and Europe. The basic question then is: can information make a contribution to such massive complex problems, and if so, should information campaigns be organized differently in Third World settings to contribute to these distinct needs? The answer is: yes, information campaigns should be organized distinctly in the South, given national economic, political and cultural realities, the national analysis of underdevelopment, and the nation's selection of its development path. Unfortunately, many national development plans continue to be economic and technological exercises that presently do not deal with questions of national transformation, class, culture, and power that cut across sectors, e.g., agriculture, health. This compartmentalized conceptualization of development into agriculture, health, etc., leads to a complementary conceptualization of development-support communication campaigns into agriculture-extension and health education. The planners at the top decide what is good for the nation, in each sector, and the grass roots must be encouraged to comply. This is the role assigned to information campaigns—to make audiences see the wisdom of the state's thinking so they will do what they are told to, namely, become cultivators of high-yielding varieties of grain who plan their families and immunize their children.

Do we have evidence that Western theories of communication can help media producers to inform, educate, and motivate? The answer is yes. Do we have evidence that Western theories of persuasive communication can get Third World audiences to do what their planners want, without giving the people a role in deciding whether it is in their self-interest? The answer is no.[16]

Notes and References

1. Osmo Wiio. 'Time and Information: Intercultural Aspects of Human Communication'. Paper presented at the World Communications Conference, Athens, Ohio, 1979.

2. The most influential theory has been the two-step flow of communication presented in Elihu Katz and Paul F. Lazarsfeld. *Personal Influence*. New York: The Free Press, 1955. Also see Joseph T. Klapper. *The Effects of Mass Communication*. Glencoe, IL: The Free Press of Glencoe, 1960.

3. For details on the effects of the mass media, see Shearon Lowery and Melvin de Fleur. *Milestones in Mass Communication*. New York: Longman, 1983.

4. Donald F. Roberts and Nathan Maccoby. 'Effects of Mass Communication', in Gardner Lindzey and Elliott Aronson, ed. *Handbook of Social Psychology*, vol. 2. New York: Random House, 1985.

5. Albert Bandura. *Social Learning Theory*. Englewood Cliff, NJ: Prentice Hall, 1977.

6. William J. McGuire. 'The Myth of Massive Media Impact: Savagings and Salvagings'. *Public Communication and Behavior*, 1. New York: Academic Press, 1986.

7. See note 4.

8. T. Lindlof. 'Media Audiences as Interpretive Communities', in J. Anderson, ed. *Communication Yearbook 11*. Newbury Park: Sage, 1988.

9. D. Morley. *Family Television: Cultural Power and Domestic Leisure*. London: Comedia, 1986.

10. William J. McGuire. 'Theoretical Foundations of Campaigns', in Ronald E. Rice and Charles K. Atkin, eds. *Public Communication Campaigns*. Newbury Park, Sage, 1989.

11. C. Hovland, I. Janis, and H. Kelly. *Communication and Persuasion*. New Haven, CT: Yale University Press, 1953.

12. George McBean. *Re-thinking Visual Literacy: Helping Pre-Literates Learn*. Nepal: UNICEF, 1989.

13. Mary Field Belenky and others. *Women's Ways of Knowing: The Development of Self, Voice and Mind*. New York: Basic Books, 1986.

14. Michael Ray. 'Marketing Communications and the Hierarchy of Effects', in P. Clarke, ed. *New Models for Mass Communication Research*. Beverly Hills: Sage, 1973.

15. Richard E. Petty and John T. Cacioppo. *Communication and Persuasion: Central and Peripheral Routes to Attitude Change*. New York: Springer Verlag, 1986.

16. S. Luis Ramiro Beltran. 'Farewell to Aristotle: "Horizontal" Communication'. *Communication*, 5, 1980.

HOW TO RESEARCH THE AUDIENCE 6

The need for audience participation in mass media use for national transformation has been mentioned in many non-governmental and governmental speeches and publications. This book focuses on one way of actually doing it: how to elicit

audience participation in message design for community participation in national transformation. Pioneering production efforts
have involved scriptwriting, acting, artwork, and camera work by
the community audience. Systematic audience research is proposed
as an additional participatory mechanism at the *preproduction
design* stage and then again at the midproduction stage to ensure
that message design implementation accurately represents people's
wishes and communication preferences. It goes without saying that
uninhibited, unconstrained, frequent audience input is desirable
for mass media message design that represents audience interests.
While audience participation in national transformation media use
is an end in itself, participatory audience research is also a means
to an essential end—achieving communication through the mass
media. Message designers for national development need to know
three things, irrespective of the medium, topic, or country where
they work:

1. What does this audience that the message is representing
   and speaking to already know, want to know, and need to
   know?
2. What forms of communication are indigenous to this community, e.g., what channels, words, images, and gestures
   does this community use to communicate among its own
   members?
3. Will our draft messages get and hold attention, be understood, and actually be found useful by this audience?

The answers to these questions must be accurate if they are to
form the basis of message design decisions for national transformation. Research as an audience participation mechanism needs to
be as carefully planned as do productions based on it. Time,
money, and accuracy are important issues in both cases. Just as a
television producer and a filmmaker have shooting scripts, similarly,
the conduct of research needs a work plan, with more detail than
merely 'Reserve a vehicle for a field trip to visit villagers'. Media
producers are encouraged to research their 'topics', but few are
taught to research their 'audiences'. The following how-to chapters
use limited social science jargon so they can be useful to media
producers who may have to do their own audience research in the
absence of formally trained communication researchers on the team.

The next section offers four basic principles for preproduction and midproduction audience participation in message design for national development.

It is conventional wisdom in all attempts to collect information on audiences and topics, to:

1. Go from the known to the unknown—start with confirming existing knowledge on the audience and program topic. Then, proceed to questions you know nothing about. Talk to those who have spent time investigating answers to the questions you have in mind.

2. Go from the general to the particular—start with observing the total situation in which the community lives, e.g., how land and capital resources are distributed. Then proceed to details. Observations will save the team from asking unnecessary questions and point toward relevant subsequent questions about why people behave the way they do.

INFORMATION COLLECTION GUIDELINES

1. Observe and Listen to a Carefully Selected Sample Genuinely Representative of the Intended Audience

Probability and sampling theory demonstrate how listening to a small number of carefully selected members of the intended audience can provide an acceptable idea of the characteristics of *all* its members. It is important that the number and kinds of people selected in the sample be actually representative of the intended audience, if the message is to communicate with them.

The simplest message design situation is when the intended audience is homogeneous, e.g., small farmers who are similar to each other in the languages they speak, the crops they cultivate, and the size of their holdings. The reality of communication via the mass media is more complex: even 'small' media like local radio stations that cover a small land area actually reach a range of small farmers. Like every other occupational group, small farmers differ among themselves. These differences may be due to differences in age, sex, caste, tribe, religion, economic status, who their friends and advisors are, what media they are exposed to, and a whole host of other factors. If a production team is hoping to communicate with *all* these different segments in the same message or series of messages, it must first listen to a representative few from each segment to understand *if* they differ among themselves on media exposure, preferred communication treatment of the topic, e.g., raising pigs for supplementary income. If initial investigations indicate that they do differ, the team will need to interview a sample of twenty-five to thirty-five people from each major segment to get a good understanding of the different perspectives in each segment. The differences may be inconsequential on this topic, and hence justify a single series of messages, perhaps with different component parts. There is always the possibility that the differences dictate separate messages/materials/media for each segment. The development agency (government or voluntary) will then calculate whether the benefit of separate messages (better chances of achieving communication) is greater than the added cost. The team should ensure that the separate strategy for each group does not have negative effects on the others, if there is an overlap in exposure.

Sampling systematically in multiple stages (e.g., villages first, then households, then individuals) helps achieve *representation* of the diversity of the audience population. The person doing the research should first circle on a map the physical area where the selected media audience lives. The next step is to write down the names of all the villages (residential settlements) from the map. If the primary concern is reaching small farmers in rural areas, ponder the following: will differences in geography, religion, or gender of the farmer (or any other factor) cause the intended audience of small farmers to differ in their response to the message? If *regional* factors cause significant differences in the responses of individual farmers, divide the residential areas into regional segments. If culture is a significant factor, divide farmers into different *cultural* segments. Sample from each segment. This stratification into clusters helps guarantee representation of crucial differences within the small farmer sample that the producer will dialogue with before and during production. The researcher on the production team is now ready to sample villages and then individual small farmers from each cluster/segment, in multiple stages.

2. Beware of Bias in Who You Listen to

How to select villages and then farmers from each cluster without showing a natural human bias towards approaching nearby villages or people most like oneself who are easiest to talk to? How to phrase questions so the audience knows that honest answers are welcomed rather than polite agreement with the interviewer?

Let us assume time and transport resources are restricted to eight day-long audience visits. Let us also assume that the researchers find that there are four distinct segments in their intended small farmer audience. They therefore consider visiting two villages from each cluster. How should they select eight villages from among the ninety-nine villages in this cluster? The researcher needs to number each of the villages. He/she then selects any number by taking a stab at the following random numbers table blindfolded. The two-digit number (because there are no more than ninety-nine villages) closest to where the pencil lands will be Village One.

Select the second village by going up, down, left, or right from the first stab at the table, but decide on the direction, e.g., up and then left or right, or down and then right or left, *before* starting the sample selection process.

Suppose the team does not have a map of the coverage area and cannot make a list of all the communities in its radius. Suppose there is no travel time to visit randomly selected villages which could turn out to be far from headquarters and off bus routes. Such problems force researchers to be pragmatic. How should the researchers honor the twin criteria of sample representativeness and bias-free selection of individuals in attempts to learn from the audience?

Quota or convenience samples are a possible choice. In a quota sampling situation, a fixed number of villages or individuals are selected in each cluster without concern for probability issues. In convenient sampling, villages and individuals are selected from accessible locations. These approaches necessarily have the obvious weakness of not being representative of the larger population, so they must be interpreted with caution. If time permits a visit to only one village on a bus route, how should the researcher proceed? Bear in mind that communities closer to cities have more exposure to information, education, and visitors from the outside world than communities which are further away. Why not purposively pick the

TABLE 6.1   RANDOM NUMBERS

1862	3250	8614	5683	6757	5628	2551	6971
3028	2338	5702	8819	3679	4829	9909	4712
2935	1141	6398	8387	5634	9589	3212	7963
5020	6612	1038	1547	0948	4278	0020	6509
8286	8377	8567	8237	3520	8244	5694	3326
3851	5870	1216	2107	1387	1621	5509	5772
2849	3501	3551	1001	0123	7873	5926	6078
2962	1183	3666	4156	4454	8239	4551	2920
2701	2378	7460	3398	1223	4688	3674	7872
5997	0885	1053	2340	7066	5328	6412	5054
1457	8999	2789	9068	9829	1336	3148	7875
7864	4029	4494	9829	1339	4910	1303	9161
2375	2542	4093	5364	1145	2848	2792	0431
8554	6881	6377	9427	8216	1193	8042	8449
9096	0577	8520	5923	4717	0188	8545	8745
5569	0279	8951	6183	7787	7808	5149	2185
9427	8422	4082	5629	2971	9456	0649	7981
3389	4739	5911	1022	9189	2565	1982	8577
3849	4715	3156	2823	4174	8733	5600	7702
5611	4763	8755	3388	5114	3274	6681	3657
6806	2692	4012	0934	2436	0869	9557	2490
9378	7670	8284	7431	7361	2912	2251	7395
7213	1905	7775	9881	8782	6272	0632	4418
8674	9202	0812	3986	1143	7343	2264	9072
8746	7390	8609	1144	2531	6944	8869	1570
8020	9166	4472	8293	2904	7949	3165	7400
8134	9588	2915	4116	2802	6917	3993	8764
9702	1690	7170	7511	1937	0723	4505	7155
3294	2684	6572	3415	5750	8726	2647	6596
0950	0890	6434	2306	2781	1066	3681	2404
7311	5270	5910	7009	0240	7435	4568	6484
0599	5347	2160	7376	4696	6969	0787	3838
6906	9177	1492	4680	3719	3456	8681	6736
3849	4819	1008	6781	3388	5253	7041	6712
6712	9614	2736	5533	9062	2534	0855	7946
0004	5563	1481	1546	8245	6116	6920	0990
9509	0341	8131	7778	8609	9417	1216	4189
5321	3125	9992	9443	5951	5872	2057	5731
6121	8770	6053	6931	7252	5409	1869	4229
3899	2685	6781	3178	0096	2986	8878	8991

* From Donald B. Owen, *Handbook of Statistical Tables.*
Reading, Mass.: Addison- Wesley, 1962.

largest village from among the furthest, and then select small farmers from each of the different cultural and agricultural strata that might react differently? To guarantee representation from the range of different cultural and economic groups who live in different parts of large villages, randomly select farm households from each of the different residential sections of the village. This is one way to handle time and travel constraints without completely giving up on attempts to draw representative unbiased samples.

The important thing is not to select or reject a village or a person because of some bias or preference. Several other solutions are possible, in the spirit of 'randomness', depending on the local situation. On arrival in each village, use the same impersonal mechanical process to ensure that personal preferences do not bias the procedure for the selection of farmers. If there are 500 small farm families and there is time to talk to only thirty, select the sample of thirty as well by using the table of random numbers.

For preproduction and midproduction message design research, listening to twenty-five to thirty-five randomly selected members of a distinct segment in the intended audience should suffice. If no majority position or general pattern of agreement or disagreement emerges on the topic after thirty-five interviews, the researcher may want to continue interviewing, or reconsider the questions.

Personal biases and preferences express themselves in a variety of unobtrusive ways in conducting research that the team may not notice initially. When the researcher decides to go to observe a village where someone has friends who will arrange introductions to audience members, some may regard this to be a practical time-saving strategy. By doing this, the team is letting friendships determine the 'source' of information. Friends of friends will be friendly people, but they may not be typical of the intended audience. Thus, who the team talks to can also bias or distort findings.

Additionally, the kinds of questions asked of the audience, the phrasing of the questions, the topics of the questions, and the issues not included on the list of things to observe are a reflection of researcher bias. With the phrasing of a question as follows, 'Your employer looks like a nice guy. He treats his workers well, doesn't he?' the researcher is indicating a preference for a certain kind of answer. Many employees will politely agree rather than risk losing their jobs. That is a leading question, indicating a preferred answer; it illustrates biased question design.

3. Use a Combination of Information Collection Methods

It is feasible to collect data on audience knowledge, attitude, and practice through many methods, in addition to large sample surveys, as described in the next section. Some methods provide a picture of the total situation while others help to get a close-up shot of each part. Some methods present statistical descriptions, others provide qualitative insights. Some methods give depth, others provide breadth. The psychologist's and sociologist's methods are those of the outsider, different from the anthropologist who gets immersed in the community. Each method has its own limitations, so combining methods helps counteract the biases of individual methods.

4. Be Pragmatic

Audience research in the service of message design is constrained by deadlines, and the availability of budgets, just as media production is. The utility of this research depends on whether it contributes to effective communication, and not whether it qualifies for journal publication. It is better to provide some rough-and-ready insights on the intended audience's concerns, rather than have grandiose research plans that provide no help to message design for national transformation.

To summarize, the touchstones of good audience research are representation of the diversity of the audience, objectivity, the use of multiple methods of information collection, and pragmatism. Now, the production team is ready to choose which methods it will use to collect information on its audience.

INFORMATION COLLECTION METHODS

Some audience research methods yield results faster and cost less than others; others are more reliable but may take longer to complete. Time, money, and staff availability play a major role in selection of research methods. The researcher should always try

Table 6.2		
Information Collection Planning Chart		
Items of Information Needed From the Audience (list below)	Data Collection Methods	When, Where, How Many to Interview
A. What to communicate (needs)		
B. How to communicate (media, words, images, music, sets, characters, folk stories, etc)		
C. Pretest questions		

to use more than one method to understand the audience, so the strengths of one will complement the limitations of the other. How to plan? Table 6.2 presents a simple chart to plan audience participation in message design. On the left hand, the production team lists the information it needs from the audience under the '*what* to communicate' and '*how* to communicate' headings. Questions that need to be answered for midproduction testing of draft messages are the same, irrespective of the message. The researcher uses the next two columns to list which methods will be used to answer each question. Whichever methods are chosen, it is essential to ensure that the information is a valid representation of the audience's responses. National transformation efforts cannot be based on the audience researcher's biases (or those of the boss of the development agency). Some information is not better than no information, if it is inaccurate, distorted, and partial.

Once the media production team has listed questions, how should they proceed to answer them?

1. Read; talk to experienced individuals who know the community and the issues.
2. Visit representative communities to observe and listen.
3. Then formulate specific questions. Try to achieve economies of time and money by conducting group interviews first, saving only the sensitive personal *why* questions for the more time-consuming individual interviews.

Then, conduct midproduction audience pretests of messages.

1. Observe reactions to draft messages or previously produced messages, and
2. Conduct focus group discussions to pretest messages.

The following are basic guidelines on sources and methods of audience data collection:

1. Begin with Existing Information in Books, Reports, Census Documents, and Media Programs

There is no need to reinvent the wheel if national development researchers have investigated this topic/audience before. Read their findings in libraries, universities, and government offices. Anthropologists, sociologists, and social work researchers may have assessed the needs of some of the communities in a particular medium's coverage area—wny not peruse their reports on what the audience wants to know, and what their cultural practices are? Before going to the audience to collect information afresh, learn from the impacts of messages and materials that have been used in the past. This will save time, money, and mistakes, and provide clues on what to look for during field visits.

Be sure to use the guidelines mentioned earlier when reviewing previous work: does it represent the diversity of the intended audience, is it objective, are the findings biased because only one kind of data collection method was used that provides only partial insights? The quantity of acceptable previous research will determine how much new data has to be collected.

2. Interview Researchers and Activists who Work in the Community or Specialize in the Topic the Team is Going to Address

Their findings are *one* source of information to help decide what to communicate and how. Combine this advice with information received from other sources. Be skeptical about every piece of information, unless it is confirmed and supported by several sources and, ideally, by personal observation.

3. Observe the Audience before Beginning to ask Questions: Listen

Listening *attentively*, putting preconceptions aside, is not easy. It requires respecting others, recognizing their autonomy, keeping quiet. Audiences are people who live active lives, making their own decisions all day, everyday, just like media producers. The production team should pay attention to the audience, their words and stories, their conversations, speeches, songs, poems, and local publications, to understand how to communicate with them. Listening and observation as information collection methods help to describe the *general picture*. Researchers can then move from asking questions to confirming observed patterns and to making the general to the particular with inquiries about why specific practices or habits exist. Additionally, why waste the audience's time with questions about the cleanliness of pit latrines when the answer is obvious to the naked eye? First, listen and observe, and *then* ask questions.

The ideal would be to observe behavior as a participant in the daily life of the community. Such *participant* observation is the anthropologist's method and provides an *approximation* of the community's perspective. Many anthropologists argue that a minimum of several months of participant observation is critical for reliable data collection. Other anthropologists with experience in specific areas (e.g., applied health care, agriculture, nutrition, education) have become convinced that the process of gathering essential ethnographic data has to be a relatively rapid process, given time and budget constraints when planning national transformation in the Thirld World. Data from rapid ethnographic assessment is clearly inadequate for a thorough analysis of local sociocultural systems but start visits after a review of literature can provide basic information about cultural attitudes and behaviors toward a particular topic (e.g., village self-government, diarrhea).

Plan observation trips carefully: before choosing *where* to go, list *what* and *who* to observe, and plan how to observe and record observations. The more clearly structured the observation trip, the more productive it will be in answering specific questions about specific locations (e.g., farms, schools, stores, streets, homes) and specific relationships (e.g., the farmer-land relationship, the male-female relationship, the teacher-student relationship). Plan for enough leeway in terms of extra time and petrol to take in unexpected sights, sounds, and accidents. A structured observation plan with flexibility that makes allowances for shocks and surprises is good.

Be sure to observe as *unobtrusively* as possible. Do not dress and behave in a manner that might make the audience *react* to the team's presence and begin to behave differently from the way they normally would. Walk around, eat in local restaurants, drink in pubs and cafes, worship with the people, and strike up casual conversations at the bus stand: dress and behave to fit in with the local scene. The team (or its research person) is visiting the audience to learn from them, not to impress them with their 'superior' clothes and upbringing. Be as invisible as is possible for a stranger to be. This is hard for both foreign *and* domestic researchers on their first trip to a community.

Many producers, researchers, and subject specialists cannot tolerate being anonymous and invisible—they like to be greeted and hailed as 'big people' wherever they go. Some people (e.g., news presenters) may be so well-known all over that they would disturb the normal pattern of life under observation no matter how much they tried to fit in unobtrusively. Both kinds of people are liabilities and hindrances: neither should be entrusted with collecting audience data or accompanying audience research teams.

Researchers should not trust their memory to recall what they have observed. Document sights and sounds as soon as possible. Unobtrusive observation should be followed by unobtrusive documentation of observations. Some observers use tiny cameras and cassette recorders in addition to observation forms and notebooks. The richer the detail, the more information is available for scripting dialogues, choosing locally appropriate characters, and building sets.

Some communication units have developed 'field laboratories' or audience 'panels' consisting of randomly selected villages and villagers with specific characteristics. The team returns regularly to the same community when it needs information from a sample that matches its characteristics, e.g., age, sex, income, occupation, language. The returning researcher becomes a known and trusted visiting member of the community over time, and has chances of collecting lifestyle and needs assessment data that a first-time visitor could never get. Rather than starting from scratch on each visit, this system enables the researcher to build on rapport established over a period of time.

While good observation can describe reality, it may not be able to fully explain *why* things are the way they are. This leads the production team to the interview method of information collection as a logical follow-on to observation.

4. Interview Groups and Individuals in the Intended Audience to Understand the *Causes* of Attitudes and Behaviors

Transformation-oriented communication campaigns need to establish the audience's reasons for particular behaviors. Useful interviews are often a combination of fully formulated questions 'structured' in advance to be asked in a prearranged order, and loosely structured questions left to the discretion of the interviewer to formulate. Useful interviews depend on well-trained interviewers.

A. Interviews with groups of audience members should be planned around a list of *what-to-ask-about* issues where the precise wording of questions is left to the judgement of an interviewer sensitive to the local situation. Ideally, they should be drafted in the language of the community, since language is an expression of logic, premises, basic categories, thinking, sensitivities and worldview. Since a lot is lost in translation, the interviewer must be a native speaker from the community. The interviewer is then free to go *in depth* and *focus* on specific *why-and-how* issues in the lifestyle and behavior of the audience, depending on how the discussion flows. A variation on group discussions, this method of information collection is often called the *group depth* interview or the *focus group* interview. The ability to probe into community attitudes and practices with a group of community members is the strength of the group interview method. Such probing in an individual interview might make the individual very uncomfortable and lead to defensive answers rather than explanations of community attitudes and practices. The findings emerge from conversations among group members, and not from question-answer interactions between the interviewer and audience members.

Ideally, *focus group interviews should be conducted in a quiet, informal atmosphere where eight to twelve audience members from similar backgrounds* (e.g., male farmers over 50 years of age or house-bound mothers with infants) respond to the moderator's questions in a relaxed manner for one to two hours. A group that is too small may not provide the security and stimulation required for a group to discuss sensitive issues, while a large group may become unmanageable. Differences in age, sex, education, income, and occupation within a group make it more difficult for eight to twelve people to feel comfortable interacting with each other on the same wavelength. While a street corner is not a good place for an in-depth group discussion because it is noisy, a classroom with chairs may be bad because it is too formal.

The success of focus groups depends on the selection of an appropriate group discussion leader or moderator: someone who is respectful of people, good at getting strangers to talk, encouraging the quiet ones and restraining the dominating ones. The moderator must be someone who is able to rephrase questions in the vocabulary of the group at the spur of the moment, someone who is a good listener. After getting each member to introduce himself/herself, the good moderator will present anecdotes that illustrate how useful such audience participation has been for message development in the past. The moderator then introduces the questions for discussion, one after the other. The flexibility that is the strength of this information collection method depends on the availability of an appropriate discussion leader.

Group interview guidelines must be tailored to meet local conditions. The agrarian context frequently consists of men and women who go to their farms at dawn and return tired at dusk. Older children who are not in school stay home tending their younger brothers and sisters. An unplanned group interview with diverse audience members at central locations such as bus stands, stores, and health centers does not permit a sustained constructive focus. A specially organized discussion with a homogeneous group (that implies that they stay away from their fields or attend an after-dinner meeting under a kerosene lantern) sometimes requires the payment of a respectable honorarium. It is wise to take the time at the start to establish good *personal* rather than financial relations. It is preferable to schedule the visits at times that respect local work routines and use naturally occurring homogeneous groups as partners in message design for local and national development; the custom of payment for information (transferred from market research to development communication audience research) assumes a transactional relationship that is alien to notions of community self-development.

A member of the production team should be responsible for silently observing the discussion and systematically documenting the proceedings on a notepad or tape recorder. At the end of each group discussion, the note-taking observer and the moderator write a memo summarizing the group's answers to each of the quesions raised by the production team. *Discussion groups with the same list of questions should be repeated until they confirm the main findings without any shadow of doubt and generate few new insights.* Usually, a pattern begins to emerge after three to five group discussions with each homogeneous segment. It is then time to prepare a summary of the main findings per question with action-implications for program development or modification.

Group interviews can be relatively inexpensive, *quick sources of insights* but they are tricky to set up, difficult to moderate, and hard to interpret. They cannot provide accurate answers to questions such as 'how many' and 'how much' in numbers and percentages. When quantitative information is necessary, the production team should supplement the insights of the group interview method with findings from structured individual interviews with representative samples.

B. Interviews with individual members of the media audience vary in terms of their structure. They can be in-depth investigations where the interviewer phrases questions to suit individual audience members and interviewees are free to respond in their own words. Or, they may be individual interviews that use a list of standard questions for all interviewees with a fixed set of multiple answers from which to choose. The baseline knowledge-attitude-practice (KAP) survey is usually of the latter kind. In both cases, the audience researcher who wants to listen and learn must establish an interpersonal relationship in which the interviewee can feel safe and relaxed. Researchers sometimes ask **TOO MANY** questions as a result of their desire to pursue a hypothesis or reach a conclusion when interviewees prefer to talk without interruption. A structured sequence of questions may restrict the audience member from describing his/her experience in his/her own terms, just as much as an interviewer who does not understand the local culture. Some cultures consider it impolite to be negative or disagreeable to strangers, so visiting interviewers are likely to receive a large proportion of socially desirable positive answers to all questions, irrespective of the truth. In societies with high literacy rates, respondents may be expected to write their answers in a questionnaire form, but with the majority of the world's population, interviewers have to ask questions and note answers themselves on what is frequently called an interview guide or schedule.

Message design teams usually conduct individual interviews with twenty to thirty individuals who represent each audience segment, using a combination of structured and semistructured questions. The standard structured list of questions usually looks for confirmation of descriptive information on lifestyle and media habits acquired from reports, experts, observation, and group discussions. Open-ended questions aim to probe for beliefs, values, and attitudes that require privacy. Structured interviews are better at answering *what* questions about the audience rather than *why* questions. *What* questions include what the audience's weekday and weekend work schedules are, and what their joys, fears, and sorrows are. This information helps determine transmission times and display locations for posters, as also the proportion of time/space to be allocated to different topics, e.g., agriculture versus health. A typical structured question may be:

At what times in a typical day do you use newspapers, radio, and television? (Specify exact time-slots in a table below the question so the interviewer can circle it easily.)

or,

What proportion of your monthly income do you spend on: (The interviewer circles the closest percentage on a chart—see next page).

Notice that the phrasing of the question and the answer categories are fixed ('structured' in advance) to save time and guarantee standardized administration to large samples.

Descriptive sample surveys can provide definitive estimates for total populations but are expensive to undertake, consume large amounts of time, and require technical skills in sample selection, question design, and computerized data analysis. Given the high cost of doing large sample surveys, media organizations encourage production teams working on specific programs for specific audiences to turn to existing reports, documents, and censuses for basic descriptive information about the lifestyles and needs of their populations. An example of a large descriptive sample survey that a big media organization would finance might be a baseline knowledge-attitude-practice survey on family planning or AIDS, or an audience ratings study to show its financiers what its share of the media audience is, and what the demographic background of its readers/viewers/listeners is.

WHAT PROPORTION OF YOUR MONTHLY INCOME DO YOU SPEND ON:

(CIRCLE THE CLOSEST %).

FOOD	25%	50%	75%	(100%)
CLOTHING	25%	50%	75%	100%
SHELTER	25%	50%	75%	100%
EDUCATION	25%	50%	75%	100%
ENTERTAINMENT	25%	50%	75%	100%

When in-depth information on the *whys and wherefores* of audience behavior is too sensitive to be accurately obtained through group interviews, or when group interviews cannot be organized, in-depth interviews with members representing each audience segment in the media coverage area may have to be considered. A number of 'indirect' techniques based on projection are useful in obtaining sensitive information in individual interviews. One simple way is to ask audience members what they think their neighbors or friends know, feel, and do on a sensitive issue, thus permitting them to project their own views on to *third parties* like themselves without 'censoring' their answers for respectability. Another simple way of finding out if program titles and character names have the connotations that the production team wishes to conjure up, is by asking for *word associations*. The interviewer presents the audience member with a word at a time and asks him/her to name the other words that come to mind immediately afterwards. A summary of the responses from audience members will tell the scriptwriter whether the word has a happy or sad association for the audience, a hot or cold association, a colorful or a bland association, in comparison with the associations he/she wants. *Sentence and story completion tests* can be used by message design teams to understand the audience's feelings and attitudes towards a particular program topic, medium, group, government, or nation. The interviewees are asked to complete incomplete sentences such as:

'Large landowners are...
'Vaccinations cause...
'Sterilization causes...
'Today's labor are...'

Or complete stories related to the program topic such as the following:

'Two 6-year olds were out on their bicycles. One bicycle had a flat tire'.

What happened then? The writer of a series for 6-year olds may want to find out how this age group responds to such a problem before introducing any creative do-it-yourself tips. Photographs of alternative on-air presenters and cast members can be presented to a sample of the audience to check on how they are perceived in comparison with the producer's perceptions. Audience reactions to photographs and incomplete stories and sentences provide plots, words, and sentences that are extremely useful for script-writers.

To reduce the time involved in going from farm to farm conducting personal interviews in agrarian societies where domestic telephones are rare, many production teams *intercept individuals at central locations* where they gather. In a village in Asia or Africa, a good place to find women would be at the village well or stream, the marketplace, or the health center. In the Caribbean, central locations would include the post office, the church, and the rum bar. While intercepting individuals at high traffic areas saves time, the public location also implies a less private interview. The procedure for conducting individual interviews at central locations involves selecting places frequented by members of the audience and stationing interviewers there. Potential interviewees are politely greeted and invited to participate in an interview lasting a specified number of minutes. If they can spare the time required, the inter-viewer asks screening questions to ensure they fit in with criteria set for the intended audience, e.g., illiterate landless labor. The interview takes place only if the individual is a member of the intended audience for the program under development.

This chapter is the how-to-do-it heart of the book. Expect to read it several times. It has presented general and specific guide-lines on how to collect information to help message designers decide what to communicate and how to communicate. The next two chapters illustrate how to apply them.

AUDIENCE – RESPONSIVE TOPICS 7

The preceding chapters have presented pragmatic and democratic-philosophic arguments for audience-based message design. They have stressed the importance of listening to and learning from the audience, so that audience members are equal partners in designing communications for their own development. The preceding chapters have also described steps and methods for involving the media audience in the message design process, for the purpose of approximating the sender-receiver dialogue that, ideally, leads to a common understanding in everyday interpersonal communication.

As Brenda Dervin[1] has argued, information is subjective and must be treated as such by media producers. It is not a physical object that is transferred without change from sender to receiver. The processes of sending and receiving information *both* involve interpretation and hence reconstruction, modification, and recreation by the person(s) concerned. Hence, the same 'information' can mean different things to different people. This chapter focuses on how to research *what to communicate* to support the all-round development and transformation of a community, whether it is a region or a nation. The answer is obvious. The community should decide. Glamorous formats will be wasted if media content does not respond to a community's *need to know*, be it a strongly felt, lightly articulated, or as yet unarticulated need.

What information does the audience *need to know*? A need is something whose absence or lack is negative and harmful. This deficiency may be *felt* by the community *and expressed* by them. Alternatively, a need might be *observed* by a development planner, a care-provider, or a community organizer as a discrepancy between the quality of life individuals and nations *should* experience, and their *present* knowledge, attitudes, and behaviors.

Marketing communication builds on audience needs—when the audience has purchasing power to buy the particular needs-resolution product the advertiser is promoting. A good example is the advertising of infant formula to lactating mothers. Except in those rare cases when a mother cannot feed her newborn infant, breast-feeding is the best, cleanest, cheapest, and most nutritious source of infant food. Many Third World mothers have no resources to boil water or keep bottles sterile and clean. The success with which the practice of bottle-feeding has spread among lactating mothers who have no physical need to switch to bottles demonstrates how accurately the message designers diagnosed the postcolonial audience's confidence in the superiority of Western products, and how successfully they converted the need to have the best (Western products?) for one's baby into a purchasing decision in spite of the audience's limited purchasing power. In development communication for national transformation, the assumption is that the state is constituted to serve its publics, those with purchasing power *and* those without. Hence, development planners are expected to address the needs of the homeless, the hungry, and the landless, even though their needs are not backed by purchasing power or political lobbies. The reality is that Third World states have neglected to do so: nongovernmental organizations have stepped in to meet the needs of silent and poor majorities.

Media use in support of national development in Asia, Africa, Latin America, and the Caribbean is distinct from the ideal. Development initiatives are conceptualized in terms of separate watertight sectors (e.g., agriculture, health) by governments and some nongovernmental agencies, rather than in terms of the holistic development of the total person. The root causes of national underdevelopment, dependency, and individual disenchantment with the postcolonial state are not addressed as indicated in Chapter 1. 'Grow more food' campaigns harangue individuals but ignore the systemic causes of hunger (e.g., unequal distribution of cultivable land, inadequate grain warehousing facilities). The use of the media to support development initiatives is characterized by the same superficial analysis. Since analysis of underdevelopment and development is flawed, selection of topics for media support is similarly flawed. Two types of development communication situations prevail, both problematic: (*i*) Communication attempts initiated by *development* agencies—governmental and nongovernmental; (*ii*) Communication initiatives by *media* agencies, governmental and nongovernmental.

DEVELOPMENT AGENCY INITIATIVES

In communication attempts initiated by agencies primarily responsible for particular development sectors (e.g., animal husbandry, health), bureaucrats and technical experts in government (or retired bureaucrats, who frequently staff nongovernmental agencies) provide a list of topics (experts' perceptions of what the audience needs) to a media organization. *Facts For Life*,[2] published

Facts For Life
The Top Ten

1. The health of both women and children can be significantly improved by spacing births at least two years apart, by avoiding pregnancies before the age of 18, and by limiting the total number of pregnancies to four.

2. To reduce the dangers of childbearing, all pregnant women should go to a health worker for prenatal care and all births should be assisted by a trained person.

3. For the first few months of a baby's life, breast milk *alone* is the best possible food and drink. Infants need other foods, in addition to breast milk, when they are 4 to 6 months old.

4. Children under 3 have special feeding needs. They need to eat five or six times a day and their food should be enriched by adding mashed vegetables and small amounts of fats or oils.

5. Diarrhea can kill by draining too much liquid from a child's body. So the liquid lost each time the child passes a watery stool must be replaced by giving the child plenty of the right liquids to drink—breast milk, diluted gruel, soup, or a special drink called ORS. If the illness is more serious than usual, the child needs help from a health worker—and the special ORS drink. A child with diarrhea also needs food to make a good recovery.

6. Immunization protects against several diseases that can cause poor growth, disability, and death. All immunizations should be completed in the first year of the child's life. Every woman of childbearing age should be immunized against tetanus.

7. Most coughs and colds will get better on their own. But if a child with a cough is breathing much more rapidly than normal, then the child is seriously ill and it is essential to go to a health center quickly. A child with a cough or cold should be helped to eat and to drink plenty of liquids.

8. Many illnesses are caused because germs enter the mouth. This can be prevented by using latrines; by washing hands with soap and water after using the latrine and

before handling food; by keeping food and water clean; and by boiling drinking water if it is not from a safe piped supply.

9. Illnesses hold back a child's growth. After an illness, a child needs an extra meal every day for a week to make up the growth lost.

10. Children between the ages of 6 months and 3 years should be weighed every month. If there is no gain in weight for two months, something is wrong.

From *Facts For Life: A Communicator's Challenge* (see note 2).

by UNICEF, WHO, and UNESCO, is a good illustration of an unusually useful list.

What is needed is data from the audience community on *their* perceptions of the problems and of solutions. In many cases, the problem is so widespread (e.g., failure to pay agricultural wages in accordance with minimum wage laws, low consumption of green leafy vegetables) that the planner may feel there is no need for local audience research, given the magnitude of the problem: any remedial media message will help. In some cases, an agency official is confident that by virtue of his/her senior position, he/she knows what is right and good for everyone else. Exceptions to this scenario of the all-knowing bureaucrat, when they occur, are usually found in community-based private voluntary organizations or in government units far from their bureaucratic headquarters in areas where the long arm of stultifying precedents reaches only rarely. The typical media agency that receives the typical list of developing country needs has no trained personnel to study the nature of each need or how each need is felt and expressed in different parts of its coverage area. Additionally, many media professionals feel that communication is a universal process. They are trained to communicate across subjects and audiences, so why should they go out to study the local articulation of widely felt needs before designing a message? The community-oriented media writer, producer, or set designer who wants to visit the audience may find that no provision has been made for a travel budget, travel time, or transportation.

MEDIA AGENCY INITIATIVES

In general, media agency initiatives to produce development communication messages in support of agriculture, health, or social change (such as equal treatment of women) are not based on audience research. One may classify media-initiated development communication attempts into two types, based on the nature of the initiating organization.

1. *Commercial media outlets* (owned by private or state capital) may typically include a prosocial theme in a popular soap opera series or present an occasional public affairs documentary and several public service announcements. The ideal of blending a light sprinkling of development-education content into dramatic soap operas or songs with high production values has attracted attention in research and media circles.[3] The development theme sometimes ends up being a cosmetic, nonthreatening addition. It is either a barely noticeable part of the story or an opening announcement or closing statement that the audience can easily ignore (by tuning in after the opening announcement or turning the set off before the closing statement). Even though it may have monopoly, this type of media organization does not want to risk losing its large audience through consistent, strong portrayals of social change-oriented behaviors and through elaborations of issue-relevant arguments that offend dominant groups (e.g., men, property owners, a religious group, or a political party). Only discreet mentions of a prosocial theme are allowed, so as not to trouble the audience. Naturally, such cautious endeavors do not cause the viewer to question the social problem identified, to discuss it, to reach a stage of critical consciousness and then to consider change, as in Freire's pedagogy.[4] Nor do they follow the prescription of psychologists such as Albert Bandura.[5] Bandura's social learning theory has demonstrated that viewers do acquire audience-appropriate ideas, action patterns, and psychological orientations modeled in television and films when their first few attempts at using them are positive. Careful audience research to identify appropriate alternative behaviors is important, because, when shown over and over in approximately the same way, they are influential in establishing new norms or in confirming old ones. In other words, behaviors

seen repeatedly on the television or the movie screen (or in other visual folk forms) may come to be interpreted as the manner in which viewers 'should' behave towards others (e.g., women, children, or historically oppressed groups). Thus, modeling theory (derived from social learning theory) suggests that new, prosocial behavioral patterns portrayed frequently on the screen may have a cumulative effect of considerable importance. Social psychologists Petty and Cacioppo[6] point out that when the issue presented is very relevant to the audience (e.g., how women should behave in society), then audience motivation and ability to scrutinize *issue-relevant arguments* presented are higher, and the likelihood of the elaboration of arguments by the audience is greater. The resulting attitude changes lead to behavior change that is resistant to counterpersuasion.

Finally, the present 'dominant wisdom' among media effects researchers is that media messages can be *powerful* when custom-designed for carefully specified audience segments, i.e., that a 100 percent impact can be achieved on 10 percent of the audience. Given the aforementioned psychological prescriptions for impact, it is appropriate to examine whether the so-called development-oriented soap operas *repeatedly portray change-oriented behaviors for audiences to model* (as Bandura would urge) and whether they *elaborate arguments* on important issues for audiences to analyze (as Petty and Cacioppo would recommend).

At present, it seems that the only serious attempt to change the *status quo* that one can see on profit-focused media outlets is *new product advertising*. Conceptualizing, testing, and distributing marketing messages for new products costs millions of dollars. This is in distinct contrast to the low budgets and the low quality of effort invested in promoting new social norms (i.e., urging half of humanity to treat the other half with respect).

2. Government information dissemination-focused initiatives in development communication parallel the mechanical division of departments and ministries, e.g., programs on education are conceptualized separately from messages on health although they are both addressed to the same person. This is typical of civil service operations. Here, conformity with previous practice (referred to as 'precedent' in government circles) is the organizational norm. Both the civil service and the media monopoly feel that *they* know what is good for the country. Visiting poor, illiterate communities to ask for *their* opinions and perceptions is not considered worthwhile. Hence, government media systems generally have limited audience research staff who are usually assigned to collecting postexposure feedback, especially on political and/or commercial propaganda. A travel budget and in-house vehicles for needs assessments to guide in the elaboration of arguments and the development of credible role models for specific audiences is nonexistent. Organizational motivation for needs assessment (to mobilize audience communities to discuss their development problems) is low, because the performance of the unit is not evaluated either in terms of achieving communication, or of designing communications that facilitate national development. The media organization gets higher budgets on the basis of increases in output (*numbers* of programs) not on the basis of measured impacts.

Fortunately, there are exceptions to the preceding scenario. Some of the high-visibility exceptions come from special one-shot, short-term, high-visibility drives (such as Tanzania's six campaigns, including the *Food is Life* and *Man is Health* campaigns documented by Hall and Dodds),[7] or from foreign aid interventions (such as the US Agency for International Development's three-to five-year educational media projects in Nicaragua, El Salvador, Guatemala, Kenya, and Thailand, to name only a few sites). Without a doubt, there are several other such attempts being made quietly, against great odds, particularly in nongovernmental organizations all over Asia, Africa, Latin America, and the Caribbean. To make these exceptions the rule, a change is needed in the *system* of development message design and production, so that the media organization and its infrastructure is routinely characterized by:

(*a*) topic selection informed by community needs assessment;
(*b*) adequate budgets for time, transport, food, and lodging for audience research before and during production;
(*c*) organizational evaluation based on the relevance of the topic and the intensity of communication impacts rather than on the numbers of posters, puppet shows, flipcharts, videos, and radio programs produced.

The foregoing is not a plea for *additional* budgets for needs assessments in financially-constrained economies. It is a recommendation for the *reorganization* of existing media systems entrusted with national development responsibility—to increase their efficiency, effectiveness, and creativity. Conspicuous among the few ongoing audience-based systems of this kind are grass roots video and radio stations in Latin American and the Development Education Communication (DECU) of the Government of India in Ahmedabad.

DECU's 'We Won't Tolerate Your Sins Any More'

In our country, the emotional appeal of Gandhi and the scientific-rational message of Nehru have certainly created an impact. Yet, in many rural areas—where neo-feudalism yet holds sway—this impact is but a dent in the armour of the long reigning monster of exploitation.

This exploitation takes on different 'avatars' (incarnations): the landowner exploiting the labourer; the high caste exploiting the lower castes; the rich exploiting the poor; the powerful exploiting the weak; man exploiting woman. Inevitably, and especially in the rural areas, the exploitation is all the greater because the exploiter is not only the landowner (and hence the employer), but is also rich, powerful, high caste and male. Equally inevitably, the 'exploitee' is not only a landless labourer but is also 'lower' in caste, obviously poor and weak. To make matters worse, he/she is dependent on the exploiter—for employment, for loans, and for all kinds of small favours. The vicious circle of poverty-dependence-exploitation-poverty seems endless. What is more depressing is that it is widely accepted as being inevitable (even God-given), especially by the exploited.

In our explorations of communication-catalysed development, we found that the structure of society was a major barrier to true development. If 'TV for the Oppressed' was to be our slogan, we had to tackle exploitation. In attempting this, we had two major problems even at the conceptual level itself. The first is the unfortunate fact that the oppressed and exploited seemed to be not only apathetic, but even satisfied with their lot. Rather like domesticated birds with clipped wings (who prefer the 'security' of a cage), they have—through decades of bondage—been conditioned to be quite comfortable about continuing their bonded existence.

The second problem was the nature of exploitation. It was not, as we had simplistically thought, rich vs. poor or high caste vs. lower castes. In fact, each level seemed to exploit the levels below it in a well-defined hierarchy. Thus, even within the lower castes, each caste looked down upon those castes defined as being 'below' theirs, creating a 'cascade' of exploitation.

To illustrate the harm done to the lower castes because of the hierarchy of inequality by birth: the Vankars (weaver caste) in this area have been 'bonded' for life to be scavengers for the upper castes. As the Vankars were preparing for the funeral of one of their elders one day, word came that a buffalo had just died and that the Vankars were required to drop everything and remove the carcass immediately. Consistently obliging, on this occasion they could not arrive until they had finished the last rites. As they began their religious services, 15–20 armed men arrived. The Vankars were abused and physically dragged to cleanse the upper caste neighbourhood of the dead buffalo. The old man's last rites had to wait.

We had therefore to evolve a framework in which the communication intervention would begin with making people aware of their plight, and then tackling other problems, including the numerous divisions and lack of unity among the disadvantaged. 'We Won't Tolerate Your Sins Any More' is one of the many consciousness-raising series produced in Gujarati and transmitted by the Indian Space Research Organization's Development Education Communication unit to Kheda district in India every evening, since the mid-1970s. It was a series with a difference because the historically disadvantaged lower castes contributed to its concept, characters, events, scripts; they even acted out the exploitation they live with every day. Drawing on the work being done in villages by the Behavioural Science Centre of St. Xavier's (College), the goal of this K. Vishwanath series was to create awareness of unjust socio-economic structures among oppressed classes and castes, leading to self-respect, respect for others, and unity in opposing their exploitation.

Excerpts from the Foreword of *Have na saheva paap*. [8]

What criteria should artists, broadcast producers, and writers use to decide which specific topics and issues are appropriate for the audience they hope to communicate with? How should they select media topics to meet the needs of the audience?

SELECTING AUDIENCE-RESPONSIVE CONTENT

All media content ideas must pass the following *Useful? Timely? Appropriate? Simple?* test for the specific audience for whom the message is designed.

1. *Is the Content Useful?* Does the information presented to the audience have advantages over prevailing knowledge held by the intended audience? Very frequently, formative researchers find indigenous solutions in sections of the intended audience that are unknown to the rest of the audience. Horizontal communication of solutions between similar communities improves the chances of implementation. Audiences can then evaluate alternatives presented by the production team in terms of their relative advantages. These advantages could be economic (more money, land, food) or political and social (more power, community approval, status, and influence).

2. *Is the Content Timely?* Message content may be useful, but it may come either too early or too late to influence specific actions. Timeliness is particularly important to bear in mind in agricultural societies where seasons are crucial. Why present innovative harvesting practices at sowing time? Information tips should be coordinated with the timing of the activities they are intended to influence, to increase the implementation potential of the content. If infant immunization camps are to be held all over the media coverage area in June, programs and print material on the importance of immunization should be presented in May rather than in July. Similarly, media exhortations to change the power structure of society must be sensitive to the political 'seasons',

in addition to stimulating audience analysis of strategic timing, i.e., when it is time to act. The message design team must prepare the audience for the inevitable violent backlash when mobilizing the community to change the distribution of land and industrial wealth. Ethical reasoning would demand primary concern for the well-being of the audience, and provision of all relevant information to make their own decisions.

3. *Is the Information Appropriate?* Audience surveys among the poor in Santiago, Chile were used in 1976 to select topics for episodes of the radio and television drama called *Sentencia.* The plot focused on a group of altruistic lawyers who ran a legal clinic in a poor neighborhood. Audience research helped determine the appropriateness of problems and solutions presented.[9] Some cultures consider the fat baby and the fat man to be healthy and prosperous. Therefore, media content that aims at introducing low-fat diets needs to address the dangers of obesity and will hence have to deal with the prevailing 'fat is wealth and prosperity' concept.

Many useful tips require **capital, purchasing power, and a change in the power structure of society.** Recommendations in agriculture frequently call for such things as hybrid seeds, fertilizer, irrigation, and tractor rentals. The less educated, less wealthy majority in agricultural societies are most in need of supportive information. Unfortunately, they find messages designed for them often require large landholdings and significant capital for their utilization. Such media content is inconsistent with the economic status of the audience. Why use an expensive medium that reaches massive numbers to carry capital-intensive information that is appropriate only for a small capital-owning minority of the community? Such audience-insensitive uses of the media have led to the advancement of the law and a widening of information gaps between the many poor and the few rich. Programing that discriminates positively by dealing with topics useful to the many, that are redundant for the propertied classes, can help bridge the gap.[10]

Today's **media content** frequently finds itself **contradicting yesteryear's programs and posters.** The lack of comprehensive media information on the lethal implications for humans when paddy pesticides are ingested resulted in a crippling bone disease among agricultural labor families in the Malnad region of Karnataka in India. The pesticides sprayed in the paddy fields were ingested by field crabs, which are a common part of the diet of farm labor belonging to the lower castes.[11] As research and development in science proceeds, previous recommendations become obsolete, even to the point of constituting today's cautions. Fertilizers and pesticides that were recommended five years ago are now being spoken of as dangerous. The same is true for the Dalkon shield intrauterine contraceptive device. In many areas of preventive health, e.g., heart disease, schizophrenia, depression, and loneliness, there is inadequate knowledge to generate strategies that are *universally* applicable and reliable. As we advise audiences to replace their present behavior with newer practices we must recognize the confusion that contradictory advice often causes for the audience. The media specialize in the dissemination of generalizations. Presentation of 'why' information (knowledge of principles) in addition to 'how-to' information is crucial, so that audience members can decide what is appropriate for their individual conditions.

4. *Is the Information Simple?* The more complex the message content, the more difficult it is to present and to comprehend. If the information is complex, media producers should think in terms of a series with each program or poster making one or two points only. Repetition and recapitulation become crucial when dealing with complex ideas.

NEEDS ASSESSMENT

The dominant topic selection procedure for development message design consists of bureaucratic and technical experts listing their solutions to other people's problems for dissemination via the mass media. Few of these experts stop to ask about the nature of the problem, or about its root causes, as opposed to its symptoms, so that alternative solutions can be presented for the audience to evaluate. Frequently, campaigns are commissioned to deal with what is perceived as a knowledge and attitude problem, when the root cause is economic and political (e.g., national integration of different linguistic groups).

How should a production team go about generating a list of alternatives that audiences will consider useful, timely, compatible, and simple? Let us assume the production team begins with some idea about **whom** they want to communicate with (e.g., farmers) and **what** topics they want to deal with (e.g., agriculture). Such topic selection could be the result of assignment by the Ministry of Agriculture or it could be determined by the mandate of the voluntary agency or grass roots organization for which the writer, producer, and researcher work. Or it may be selected from lists, such as *Facts For Life*. In the 1970s, experiments were conducted with audio cassette listening forums. The women's group in two villages in Tanzania[12] chose five leaders from among themselves who were trained to study the needs and resources of their members. The needs were then ranked and taped dramatizations of the problems were used to elicit group discussion and development of an action plan.

A media organization committed to facilitating community development in its coverage area will begin the assessment of needs by first observing, asking questions, and listening in the community. The recommended procedure is to observe, conduct group interviews and then individual interviews in the community, to arrive at a list of high-priority problems and information needs—e.g., land to cultivate, enforcement of minimum wage laws, clean drinking water. The message design audience participation chart in Chapter 6 is a good organizational device.

Sometimes, media agencies are given a list of topics by the government or by a voluntary agency. Either way, the team should first establish what the audience knows, feels, and does on each topic, and also what *they* want to know. Existing gaps in knowledge, feeling, and behavior will be the take-off point for message design. These gaps will be the baselines that evaluators will use to measure changes triggered by exposure to media messages. An analysis of gaps (needs) will help to focus the search for appropriate solutions.

The Third World preoccupation with acquiring technology and trainers led to a neglect of *whose* knowledge should be transmitted to bridge gaps—which class, which race, which nationality, which gender. Wrong-headed faith in the neutrality of knowledge helped ignore these structural bases of inequality.

Table 7.1

Gaps Analysis

What the audience *should* know/would like to know	What the audience *actually does* know	What is the *gap*?
12 items (list)	3 items (list)	9 items (list)

Designers of needs assessment studies must recognize that audiences cannot express a need or feel a lack of the resource or solution they do not know about. Populations which have been living in poverty for generations are resigned to hurt; they articulate few demands beyond the basic minimum. Thus, visiting specialists may see a need to provide specific information (e.g., about equal pay for equal work) for which the audience may not express a need. Media content that responds to needs that are clearly felt and expressed by the audience naturally have a better chance of receiving attention. Media messages that respond to needs felt and observed only by outsiders have to first create an awareness of these needs in the audience, before they can expect the audience to attend to messages aimed at meeting these needs.

A large proportion of people around the world have been socialized into a 'culture of silence'. They have adapted themselves to the political, economic, and cultural structures of domination in which they are immersed and have become resigned to it. Media presentations of the oppressive situations in which such people live may be used to trigger community reflection, a yearning for change, and discussions about the causes of the problem, and how to transform oppressive structures. Media portrayals here are facilitators, not teachers. Many educators in the Paulo Freire tradition have used photographs, printed materials, videos, audio cassettes, and puppet shows to help peasant audiences in remote areas to start a critical dialogue with those around them on the nature of their world: who owns it, who controls it, in whose interest it functions, and what to do about it

Some community problems have no solution (e.g., AIDS); information education and communication are the only contribution. In fact, for many villages, mass media-delivered agriculture, health, and nutrition information may be their only development inputs.[13] Context-consonant interventions such as science and math education do not require any changes in prevailing social divisions of caste, class, gender, and ethnic origin and can thus make substantial contributions on their own. However, there are *basic* community problems (e.g., hunger) that are *caused* by existing power structures, and are hence not amenable to solution by media-provided information alone. Context-resistant communications need social and political organizers on site to mobilize the disadvantaged, if heightened consciousness is to lead to action. Media presentation of situations where large agricultural landowners do not pay the legal minimum wage to their labor is a political and economic intervention that is *dissonant* with the context. Televised exposes of offending landowners caused the latter to raze the huts of workers who were interviewed by the Development Education Communication Unit television crews in Kheda district in India. The landowners then led a procession to the television station to protest 'inaccurate portrayals' of landlords. The Canadian Film Board's *Challenge for Change* project used film and video to mobilize adversarial groups to speak to each other. Radio, television, audio cassettes, and video cassettes have since been used by development activists and media producers around the world, as they try to mediate between powerful decision makers and comparatively less powerful local communities. An analysis of audience needs must include an analysis of the nature of change required to meet the needs: what are the tasks, how much can the media handle alone, and how much support is needed from face-to-face channels and a responsive power structure? Dynamite is used to terrorize society, by bombing hospitals and homes. It is also used to help build bridges. Similarly, audience research methodology is a tool. Message designers can use it to address genuine audience needs (e.g., to raise healthy babies) or to put an audience-responsive *veneer* on products and services communities do not need.

This chapter has focused on establishing audience-responsive message content for development message design. The next chapter looks at audience-responsive message form and treatment: how to communicate in words and images that are familiar to the audience.

Notes and References

1. Brenda Dervin. 'Audience as Listener and Learner, Teacher and Confidante: The Sense-Making Approach', in Ronald E. Rice and Charles K. Atkin, eds. *Public Communication Campaigns*. Newbury Park: Sage, 1989.

2. UNICEF, WHO, and UNESCO. *Facts For Life: A Communication Challenge*. New York: UNICEF, no date.

3. Arvind Singhal and Everett M. Rogers. 'Prosocial Television for Development in India', in Ronald E. Rice and Charles K. Atkin, eds. *Public Communication Campaigns*. Newbury Park: Sage, 1989.

4. Paulo Freire. *Pedagogy of the Oppressed*. New York: Seabury Press, 1970.

5. Albert Bandura. *Social Learning Theory*. Englewood Cliffs, NJ: Prentice Hall, 1977.

6. Richard E. Petty and John T. Cacioppo. 'Issue Involvement Can Increase or Decrease Persuasion by Enhancing Message-Relevant Cognitive Responses'. *Journal of Personality and Social Psychology*, 37, 10, 1979, pp. 1915–26.

7. B. Hall and T. Dodds. 'Voices for Development: The Tanzanian National Radio Study Campaigns', in P. Spain, D. Jamison, and E. McAnany, eds. *Radio for Education and Development: Case Studies*. Washington, DC: World Bank, 1977.

8. S. R. Joshi *et al.* *Have na saheva paap: An Experience in Participatory Programming*. Ahmedabad, India: Development Education Community Unit, 1989.

9. Jeremiah O'Sullivan-Ryan and Mario Kaplun. *Communication Methods to Promote Grassroots Participation*. Paris: UNESCO, 1979.

10. Prakash Shingi and Bella Mody. 'The Communication Effects Gap: A Field Experiment in TV and Agricultural Ignorance in India'. *Communication Research*, 3, 2, April 1976.

11. J. V. Vilanilam. 'Rural Press for Development'. *Media Asia*, 11, 4, 1984.

12. Joyce Stanley with Alisa Lundeen. 'The Audio Cassette Listing Forum: A Participatory Women's Development Project'. Washington, DC: Office of Women in Development, USAID, 1978.

13. Robert Hornik. 'Channel Effectiveness in Development Communication Programs', in Ronald E. Rice and Charles K. Atkins, eds. *Public Communication Campaigns*. Newbury Park: Sage, 1989.

AUDIENCE – RESPONSIVE MESSAGE FORMATS 8

C hapter 6 looked at how to research audiences. Chapter 7 applied these methods to finding out the audience's needs for information, to help message designers select *topics* accordingly. The present chapter applies audience research methods to help make decisions on treatment, *form*, or presentation: which media to use, which persuasive strategies, what creative formats. The focus on presentation in this chapter might seem trivial in comparison to the life and death issues that are the substance of development. While discussion of form is not meant to detract from the primacy of content, it is important to recognize that concerns about form are not insignificant for national transformation.

The pattern of media usage in the South differs significantly from that of the more industrialized countries because media infrastructures are less developed, low incomes reduce ownership of TV sets when TV coverage is available, and low literacy limits the coverage of print media. Cinema attendance is very popular even among low income families. Trucks, cabs, and cycle rickshaws with loudspeakers are inexpensive localized small media. Given Third World resource constraints, instead of asking what is the best medium, the better question is: how to use an available medium for a specific community mobilization goal?

There are very few message formulation guidelines on persuasive appeals, format, and treatment that hold for all audiences and all topics. Simple content and active audiences are two often-repeated tips.[1] While keeping the content simple is easily understood (although not as easy to do), what should the media producer do to involve an audience on the receiving end of a one-way medium that does not have provision for talking back? Audience involvement in defining their own needs for information is primary in development communication. Entertainment programs use sex and violence to get emotional involvement. Some programs build pauses around questions directly addressed to the audience to generate mental activity. Other programs actually require physical activity, e.g., children's programs that ask their audiences to count aloud, solve a math problem, sing, jump, and exercise to music. Dervin suggests two other strategies: make the prescribed actions real for the individual viewer by connecting it to his/her personal life, and make sure the messages are repeated frequently so as to become part of the individual's stored understanding of the world.[2]

In Alice's Wonderland, Lewis Carroll's Humpty Dumpty says, 'When I use a word, it means just what I choose it to mean—neither more nor less'. In the real world of different subcultures and failures to communicate, production teams know that they do not have the power of Humpty Dumpty: the same word means different things to different people. Basic questions on *how to communicate* are: what are the audience's media habits? What words and gestures are appropriate? Which characters have high credibility? What settings can the community identify with? What message structure will motivate this particular audience to reflect on this content and discuss it with neighbors—should positive appeals that emphasize rewards be emphasized or negative appeals (such as fear) that depict the negative consequences of ignoring the issue? How should message designers organize arguments to ensure reflection: should both sides be presented and, if so, should the pros precede the cons? Should the recommended conclusion be explicitly stated or should the audience be left to draw their own conclusions?[3] Is a talking head presenting a lecture better than a televised group discussion? Should the discussion be restricted to experts or should it be a discussion among typical audience members? Should a drama be used or a folk song and dance from the traditional culture?

Much human behaviour is learned vicariously by observing others. When the occasion presents itself, this learning serves as a guide for action. What should production teams do to capitalize on observational learning?[4] Answers to each of the preceding questions depend on the audience, the topic, and objective. Obtaining the answers is achieved by going to the intended audience to find out.

Communication occurs most frequently and easily between individuals who are alike or *homophilous*.[5] *Homophily* is the degree to which pairs (e.g., the sender-receiver pair) who interact are similar in certain attributes (e.g., attitudes, knowledge, behaviors). What are the chances of communication occurring when the sender is an educated upper middle class media producer who lives in the city and the receiver is an agricultural laborer in a village with a couple of years of primary schooling, strong religious beliefs, and no contact with the urban world? Very slim. Most mass media productions are attempts to communicate across the homophily boundary with receivers very different (heterophilous) from the production team in technical competence, social status, and views on the world. This leads to the production of messages inconsistent with the receiver's language and existing beliefs that then go unheeded.

Since homophily promotes communication between people with similar backgrounds and life-experiences, it is logical that community media systems be set up in regional districts and provinces and be staffed by local staff trained on the job. Centralized media systems that try to reach remote populations with city-based producers, writers, artists, and subject experts embody heterophily and are therefore a waste of money. Until such time as community media systems are implemented with message senders and message receivers drawn from similar populations, production team members in large media production bureaucracies will have to take time to learn about their readers, listeners, and viewers—who are distant and different from them—*if they want to communicate*.

AUDIENCE LIFESTYLE PROFILE

Who is the 'invisible audience'? An analysis of the lifestyle of the audience becomes central when frequent dialogue between sender and receiver is impossible. A media organization or a development agency specializing in serving the information needs of a particular community (e.g., rural women) needs to prepare a major lifestyle profile of the audience at the beginning of the venture. It can then update this audience analysis on a smaller scale every year.

What Every Message Designer Should Know About Her/His Audience

Anthropologists focus on ethnographic cultural factors, sociologists look at the organization of groups and their relationships to each other, economists look at assets and income and how to increase them, and political scientists look at the organization and distribution of power. All these dimensions must be included in the briefing to the production team since individuals are not only economic, political, cultural, or sociological actors, but all of these simultaneously. Assume that a program topic has just been assigned to a radio producer. He/she is told he/she has to produce a weekly radio program for adult rural women. What should he/she want to find out about the audience's lifestyle and values to help decide on the media mix, message frequency, and treatment of programs? The first thing the message designer should do is make a list of audience characteristics he/she wants to know about. This should be entered in the planning chart in Chapter 6. The following list is an illustration.

A producer of women's media programs would generally list the following questions to help her/him communicate:

What is the distribution of **age** among rural women in this community? What is the nature of conjugal relations: what is the distribution of marital status versus visiting relations? What are the local implications of each? Do men migrate for jobs and schooling, leaving women behind? What are the implications of women-headed households for program treatment: would dramatic portrayals of two-parent households be ruled out, if women audience members are expected to 'model' women portrayed on the screen? Do women live longer than men and thus need special advice on the problems and challenges of widowhood?

What is the distribution of **caste, tribe**, and **race** in the coverage area? Is the role of women and their work responsibilities very different in each of these different sub segments?

What is the role of **religion** in determining the role of women? Are there any liberating role models in their religious scriptures and folk stories that can be used in programing?

What about the **economic status** of women in different social groups? How much of what kinds of work do they do? For what remuneration? What is their daily work schedule? Are the higher income groups more restrictive of the freedom of their daughters outside the home than lower income families whose daughters and sons work outdoors in similar fashion? Did women in this region have greater control over the land than they presently do because of development projects that are training only the men with the new farm machinery?

What about **literacy**? What proportion of women are literate in comparison to men? Are younger women being sent to school in increasing numbers or are they still denied the opportunity? With literacy comes the ability to decode pictures, maps, graphics, and symbols. Many posters for illiterate audiences have erred by using symbols that particular cultures were not familiar with, e.g., the use of a protective umbrella over a family has been perceived to mean that an umbrella is a substitute for an injection, medicine, and even contraceptives, depending on the nature of the problem with which the poster was dealing.

Which **media** are women exposed to? Are there some times that are more suitable than others for women of different age groups? Is the quality of exposure, attention, and distraction different in different places and times?

What are the **supportive networks** that women rely on when they need advice and help? What is a typical day in the life of a woman at different stages in her life cycle—daughter, student, teenager, bride, wife, mother-in-law, and widow—in different tribal, religious, and economic class groups?

What are the **traditional forms of education and entertainment** found in the major segments of the coverage area? In which ones do women predominate? Are there any women's songs, women's heroines, and women's deities that could be used in programs?

What norms on **appropriate behavior for women** prevail in this particular economic, political, and cultural setting of the region?

Answers to these questions will help define the lifestyle of audience segments, the media that will reach them at a suitable time and place, sources of information credible to them, appropriate characters and role models, and the kinds of locales that constitute realistic settings.

How Should Answers to Audience Lifestyle Questions be Obtained?

To make the best use of audience research time, transport, and staff resources, combine data collection on *how to communicate*, with data collection on *what to communicate*. Review Chapter 6 at this point. The guidelines are: read everything about this audience. Talk to those who have worked with them. Visit them to observe and listen. Conduct group interviews, and end with personal interviews. This method helps the message designer to learn from previous researchers. It saves the message designer from collecting fresh data every time, and it saves the audience from answering the same questions for different development planners many times over. Additionally, the use of multiple methods of collecting data helps reduce the bias of one observer or one method.

How Should Answers to Audience Lifestyle Questions be Presented?

Research reports are for researchers who read academic journals. Media producers prefer short direct answers to their questions. If the media producer and writer did not visit the audience themselves, the audience researcher might want to list answers to each question and prepare an additional note highlighting action-implications of this lifestyle data for producers. This note should list the range of local ideas, concepts, stories, characters, potential 'models', appropriate settings, dialects, music, sounds, and availability-use of the mass media for different segments of the community. Media producers welcome photographs and audio cassettes from the field that supplement the written document. Tapes of conversations would provide facts and the sounds of accents.

What formative researchers will discover when they start collecting data on the audience community is that audiences exposed to each medium (radio, posters, television) differ among themselves. All radio listeners are not *homophilous* with each other. Under the radius of the same transmitter in the same part of the country, and in the readership area of the same newspapers, reside owners of large pieces of agricultural land and those with no land, members of different tribes and religions, people of different occupations, supporters of different political parties, and a range of age groups. *All* these different groups may constitute the total intended audience that a production team may want to communicate with on an issue that is relevant to *all of them* (e.g., the common cold). Some forms of presentation may cut across these differences, but in many cases, different tones of voice and techniques will be required to get the attention of different segments within tne intended audience.

What if the audience is not homophilous? *Audience segmentation* is the process of dividing up the intended audience on the basis of similarity in response to an item crucial to achieving an identity of meaning between sender and receiver, e.g., the topic, the medium, audience demographics or psychographics. Several companies in technologically advanced countries have been selling audience segmentation services that look at demographics (such as age, sex, income) and the products that particular demographic groups purchase, along with their psychographic characteristics, such as attitudes and values. The SRI Values and Lifestyle Program designed by a California research company questions consumers on a thirty-item questionnaire and then divides them into three basic groups: the need-driven, the outer-directed, and the inner-directed. Within the three basic segments are nine diverse subsegments structured in a hierarchy. This data base helps media producers design messages that have better chances of communicating with their intended audiences. In Third World settings, many development communication message designers who work on life and death issues continue to think of themselves as instinctive communication artists who do not need the help of audience research.

Media production teams working on development communication with limited budgets need to think in terms of **audience segmentation** on two basic dimensions: (*i*) the topic of the message, e.g., stop smoking and (*ii*) exposure to the medium. The sophisticated planner with a large budget can afford to think in terms of several additional segments. He/she can then design separate series of programs in different formats for each audience segment. Media producers in some settings may have to think in terms of a single message that is designed to reach several audience segments simultaneously, by having characters and perspectives from each of the different audience segments built into a single program.

Production teams will need to segment audiences on the basis of their knowledge, attitudes, and practices related to the topic.

If communicating the advantages of eating green vegetables is the topic, people with negative attitudes and incorrect knowledge may constitute one segment while those with positive attitudes may constitute another. Multinational and Third World cigarette manufacturers segment their audiences so they have separate campaigns aimed at women, and separate campaigns aimed at men. Campaigns for adults are separate from the messages tailored for teenagers. The form and treatment of each series of messages is different to ensure communication and sales promotion. Would that media producers purveying healthy practices had access to similar budgets. Since development communication message designers frequently lack big budgets, they have to compensate through creativity (which this book does not teach) and systematic methodology (which this book does).

Another basic dimension for audience segmentation is **media literacy** and **media exposure**. Development communications planners need to ask questions such as: which medium is the right one to reach people who cannot read? Which people own working transistor radios with batteries? Which people can afford the price of a movie ticket and bus fare to the movie theater in the city? Does this audience perceive pictures and illustrations differently from media producers? An audience may be homophilous on the topic but may be heterophilous in its media skills and media access, dictating the need for using different media and different production formats on the same topic.

HOW TO COMMUNICATE

In 1989, companies around the world spent $240 billion on media advertising.[6] The nature and number of media channels are proliferating—from more television stations to advertising within public lavatories, books, and school broadcasts. Clients who have hired advertising agencies include the Governments of South Africa and the Philippines who want a good press in the United States, the Catholic Bishops Conference of America who want to try nontraditional methods of convincing their membership to adhere to traditional family planning practices, and Third World governments promoting condoms.

Once audience lifestyle data is in, the first question development communicators need to ask is *which media*: which combination of media will help their client—governmental or grass roots nongovernmental—to reach out to the constituency they want to work with? In metropolitan commercial centers, computer-based media planning models are beginning to be used for commercial campaign planning, where there is a choice of media. In rural areas, where the majority of the Third World's population still lives, availability and access to media are primary determinants: radio reaches the largest number of people, followed by print and television, depending on local literacy, electrification, and television availability. Thus, media-based development communications have no relevance for a large proportion of Third World populations who are beyond the reach of any electronic or print medium.

The second set of decisions that a production team must make relates to how to capture and hold an audience's attention, guarantee comprehension, and elicit reflection and community discussion. What does a willow or a male loin cloth in the doorway means in rural Sri Lanka?[7] Knowledge of the local culture can help in the selection of symbols, and in the use of locally-rooted ideas, concepts, story lines, characters, sets, and media channels.

Preproduction audience analysis provides essential directional signposts that no message designer can do without. However, two producers with different creative repertoires may receive the same guidelines, (e.g., a humorous appeal on an issue for X audience) and design completely different messages with widely divergent results. The provision of cultural, economic, and political profiles cannot *guarantee* the design of development messages that meet their goals. This is why midproduction testing of draft programs, ideas, and characters (discussed in Chapter 10) is so useful.

The common perception of development communications designed by Third World governments is that they are dull and boring, in addition to being official propaganda. They often are. Striking exceptions are the attention-getting songs on AIDS produced by African governments and the records and music videos produced in Latin America and the Philippines against teenage pregnancy.[8] Do government message designers give a damn? Do Third World governments assume the nonprofit public service content will attract attention in and of itself because of its substantive purity? The result is that nonprofit development messages go unnoticed. What is to be done? Once a social, economic, cultural, and political profile of a community audience is prepared, message designers should use it as the take-off point for unrestrained brainstorming for ideas on media selection and identification of creative strategies. Commercial advertising practitioners talk in terms of creative strategies more often than development communicators. Steeped in social-psychological literature, communication researchers write of persuasive strategies (e.g., instilling confidence and motivation, involving the persuadee, reasoning, fear)[9] and forces that energize or drive an audience[10] to process a communication (e.g., cognitive stability and growth, affective stability and growth). *Creative strategy* is the formulation of a new combination of old elements into a message that highlights its problem-resolution characteristics. **Creativity is not capital-intensive. It requires imagination and intelligence, items that are not in short supply in the Third World.** Commercial communications have generated several 'creative strategies' in the last forty years. In the 1940s, the 'Unique Selling Proposition' (USP) strategy was dominant in advertising circles. A USP is an offer to an audience that no one else is presently making. In the 1950s and 1960s, strategy development focused on 'image'. Irrespective of the physical qualities of a brand, the advertising emphasized its unique psychological benefits, e.g., pride of ownership. In the 1970s, the creative strategy approach was 'positioning': advertising must link the product or service to needs in the minds of the audience. What of nonprofit development communications? Many of them are using advertising techniques. A mixture of entertainment and education in development messages has become increasingly popular. Such messages attract large audiences, can pay for their costs through advertising they carry, and inform a large audience about an educational issue. As a result, they get repeated play like any other entertainment show, e.g., the rock music video which promoted sexual abstinence and contraception. *Cuando Estenios Juntos* became Number One on the popcharts in Mexico and was among the top-rated songs in eleven other Latin American countries.[11] Note, however, that each of the advertising strategies described earlier assumes a situation where the message is fighting against other messages in a competitive marketplace. When designing development communications, the competition is not from alternative and competing products or services, but from the *status quo*. The individual's past experience *and* present social, economic, political, and cultural surroundings are generally not supportive of change. Third World contexts are frequently characterized by a patriarchal society that subjugates women, an authoritarian political regime, and an economic class structure where the minority control agricultural land, industry, and jobs. When media forms *reflect* cultural reality, they frequently support this status quo. Todd Gitlin[12] has identified how the narrative action in television and dramatic films (e.g., the Hindi movie industry) uses standard characters to deal with a new version of a standard situation in episode after episode. All of these regularities of the repeated formula demonstrate continuation of the same social system and how impervious it is to change. Similarly, message forms that do not encourage the audience to question, argue, and discuss problems with each other reinforce isolation and passivity. Message designers need to innovate creative strategies and forms to activate communities to reflect on possibilities for change.

This section identifies a range of low-cost creative modes and appeals that the development communicator needs to pretest for specific contextual compatibility and community mobilization potential. The illustration of the use of audio cassettes in Iran is worth repeating: a population disenchanted with the Shah shared tapes and mimeographed sheets of Ayatolla Khomeini's speeches. A few small-scale attempts at agricultural information dissemination via tapes have been made by the Food and Agriculture Organization of the United Nations. Although academics remain skeptical, self-help audio cassettes containing subaudible messages (usually with an audible self-hypnotic version on the second side) have started selling very well in some countries. The subliminal side consists of sounds from nature (e.g., the ocean). The audible level, meant to be self-hypnotic, repeats the message in soft tones. The content includes subjects such as smoking cessation, losing weight, housecleaning, gardening, and cancer remission. Johns Hopkins University's Population Communication Services have encouraged the use of education-entertainment strategies for development, such as television drama in Nigeria and Egypt, and rock music in the Philippines and Mexico. The use of placements and tie-ins in commercial feature films by development agencies remains unexplored, unlike their frequent use by commercial advertisers of products.

An illustration of the use of audience lifestyle data in selection of formats is the diarrhea-prevention attempt in Islamic Gambia. Building on the traditional practice of soliciting Koranic verses from an *imam* to prevent particular diseases, message designers requested *imams* to prepare diarrhea-prevention messages for broadcast use. While small puppet troupes, folk artists, advertisers, and entertainment media have used India's Hindu *epics* for long-lasting effect, no similarly long-run national use has been made of this deep-rooted cultural heritage for development communication. Instead of expensive animation for children, video cameras have been used to 'read' illustrated storybooks. This *storybook animation via video* has the camera moving from spot to spot, focusing on objects described by an offscreen narrator. Thus, children between 3 and 6 years who have problems with full animation are able to see what is being described simultaneously, ensuring word-image coordination. While promoting reading readiness, this method also provides exposure to books for those income groups who would not otherwise have access to them. Formats such as comic books popular with a wide range of children and adolescents, and *photonovellas* and *telenovellas* for adults, merit more experimentation as entertaining vehicles for educational tasks. The challenge lies in perfecting the ideal combination of education and entertainment, so the integrity of neither is compromised. Again, this is a role for pretesting (Chapter 10).

Figure 8.1 shows the creative use of crossword puzzles to teach basic information on AIDS for school children. The popularity of computer games has led to the design of AIDS education games for adolescents (see Box on BLOCKAIDS). Local versions could be developed in Third World settings where some high schools have computers (and award-winning computer hackers!). As an attention-getting device, nude announcers present post-prime time programing on Manhattan cable TV: they discuss serious politics and trivia like any other TV station, but in the nude. One department of public health mailed out its media releases in a box that said: 'Look what the Department of Public Health is serving for breakfast'. Inside the box was a broken cigarette and a condom to announce the inauguration of the state's AIDS Prevention and Anti-Smoking Campaign. Except for a lighthearted, upbeat approach to safe sex information in Trinidad and Thailand, in most countries AIDS prevention communications use fear, morality,

YES! AIDS IS A PUZZLE   Figure 8.1

ACROSS

1. A steady or _____ relationship between two is the best protection against AIDS (6)
5. The transmission of this disease in America is mainly _____ (10)
6. One can die of AIDS, hence it is a _____ disease (6)
7. AIDS cannot be spread by bites from these insects (10)
11. AIDS is caused by this agent (5)
13. Use of condom, restricting sexual partners & not exchanging body fluids are examples of (4,3)
14. This is one of the early symptoms of the disease (6,4)

DOWN

2. This giver is not at risk of AIDS (5,5)
3. A _____ is at a higher risk of getting & spreading this disease (10)
4. Sexual intercourse by this route is particularly risky (4)
8. AIDS is not transmitted by using the same _____ (8)
9. One cannot get AIDS by diving into this collection of water (8,4)
10. People who are infected often look well and unaware (Right/wrong)
12. Infected men can spread this disease through ____ (5)

ACROSS (Contd.)

16. Men & Women can reduce the risk of AIDS by using this protective shield (6)
17. This important constituent of body gets infected by AIDS (5)
18. Infected mothers can pass this disease to her unborn child during _____ (9)
21. An _____ gets this disease from the mother (6)
22. Infected women, during sex pass the disease through _____ fluids (7)

DOWN (Contd.)

14. AJDS is curable (Right/wrong)
15. Skin to skin _____ does not spread AIDS (7)
19. Drug addicts sharing this are specially at risk (6)
20. AIDS is neither a water borne nor a _____ borne disease (3)

Prepared by S. Chowdhury, Center for Community Medicine, All India Institute of Medical Sciences, New Delhi, India.

and an appeal to family values. The skull and cross bones are frequently used symbols. Is this symbol understood, and if so, does the audience analysis indicate that fear is the most persuasive appeal? The use of a little fear for attention-getting followed by problem-solving advice to resolve the tension is generally acceptable. But, in the case of AIDS, the only advice is risk-avoidance or prevention. For the infected, the only hope is postponement of the onset of the disease: will the use of fear help or merely lead to denial?

BLOCKAIDS

BLOCKAIDS is an exciting, fun-to-play, AIDS education game designed to appeal to adolescents and young adults. BLOCKAIDS puts the information in the US Surgeon General's Report on Acquired Immune Deficiency Syndrome into a computer-game format. Its goals are to increase knowledge about AIDS and promote healthier AIDS-related attitudes and behavior. BLOCKAIDS is designed to break the ice, get adolescents talking, and promote communication with knowledgeable adults. It's fun to play, motivates repeated play, and promotes retention. BLOCKAIDS is a natural companion to existing AIDS resources, or serves independently. It can be used to introduce the sensitive topic, for review, for practice, for students to test their knowledge about AIDS, or just for fun. Another real plus: BLOCKAIDS immediately evaluates its own impact by keeping track of player responses before, during, and after play, quickly showing gains in awareness and changes in attitudes about AIDS.

BLOCKAIDS is based on a tic-tac-toe or 'Hollywood Squares'-like concept. It's a combination fast-action video game and quiz show, where players score points, learn about AIDS, and complete rows of blocks by answering questions about AIDS. Correct answers block the 'AIDS virus'. If the player isn't quick enough, or gets the wrong answer, the AIDS virus zaps the block, and blocks completing the row. The object is to get the highest score while players learn that knowledge pays off in the fight against AIDS.

The AIDS Threat to Adolescents

Former US Surgeon General C. Everett Koop said in his Foreword to the *Report on Acquired Immune Deficiency Syndrome* (1986) that adolescents and preadolescents 'are those whose behavior we wish to especially influence because of their vulnerability when they are exploring their own sexuality (heterosexual and homosexual) and perhaps experimenting with drugs. Teenagers often consider themselves immortal, and these young people may be putting themselves at great risk.'

Reaching the Adolescent

AIDS: A Guide for Survival and the Surgeon General's *Report on Acquired Immune Deficiency Syndrome* are excellent and authoritative materials. However, adolescents may not always see traditional forms of health education, informational health pamphlets, medical campaigns, school education programs, and so forth, as interesting and may not read or fully understand them. There's a need for additional AIDS information sources. As Dr. Eileen Starbranch, Medical Director of the Children's Unit, Belle Park Hospital in Houston has said, 'Information about AIDS prevention must be presented on multiple occasions and in many formats by sources credible to young people.'

BLOCKAIDS presents the information in the Surgeon General's Report on AIDS in a format designed to grab and hold attention, take the edge off the intensity of the subject, quickly introduce the critical information, and reduce 'head-in-sand' behavior about AIDS. It's designed to be fun and exciting—an educational game that can be played for just a few minutes·at a time or for hours. AIDS facts are presented in brief easy-to-read chunks. The game encourages repeated review and promotes retention of the facts about AIDS. If desired, built-in, before and after testing capabilities allow immediate evaluation of game-play impacts on what the player knows about AIDS, attitudes about AIDS, and how the player might handle potential AIDS risks.

Why BLOCKAIDS Will Help

The computer-game format is an innovative one for AIDS education. On the other hand, such formats have been used effectively with other sensitive topics (e.g., the cancer game simulation—Killer T-Cell). A considerable body of research has explored the use of games in the classroom. That research indicates that learning games: (*i*) involve students more than traditional teaching methods, (*ii*) motivate students and create greater interest, (*iii*) create improved student attitudes, (*iv*) increase attendance, and (*v*) affect attitude change.

The Authors

The authors are experts in the development of health-related teaching, training, learning materials. Dr. Craig W. Johnson and Wm. J. Fetter are faculty members in the Program in Biomedical Communications (BMC) at the University of Texas' School of Allied Health Sciences in Houston, Texas.

This chapter has focused on the appearance or form of development communications. It has presented audience analysis data as the basis of decisions on how to communicate. The next chapter focuses on combining topic selection and treatment into a coherent strategy and objectives.

Notes and References

1.   Godwin Chu and Wilbur Schramm. *Learning from Television: What the Research Says*. Washington, DC: National Association of Educational Broadcasters, 1979, fourth edition.

2.   Brenda Dervin. 'Audience as Listener and Learner, Teacher and Confidante: The Sense-Making Approach', in R. Rice and C. Atkin, eds. *Public Communication Campaigns*. Newbury Park: Sage, 1989.

3.   A good discussion of findings may be found in P. Zimbardo et al. *Influencing Attitudes and Changing Behavior*. Menlo Park, California: Addison-Wesley, 1977. Also see William J. McGuire. 'Theoretical Foundations of Campaigns', in R. Rice and W. J. Paisley, eds. *Public Communication Campaigns*. Beverly Hills: Sage, 1981.

4.   Albert Bandura. *Social Learning Theory*. New Jersey: Prentice Hall, 1977.

5.   Everett M. Rogers. *Diffusion of Innovations*. New York: The Free Press, 1983.

6.   'The Advertising Industry'. *The Economist*, 9 June 1990, p. 73.

7.   L.P. Medis. 'Communication in Rural Sri Lanka'. *Media Asia*, 17, 3, 1990.

8.   Johns Hopkins University has led the way in using the education through entertainment ('enter-educate') concept in a variety of media—The Tatiana and Johnny project in Latin America, the Lea and Menudo project in the Philippines, and the King Sunny Ade and Onyeka Onwenu project in Nigeria.

9.   Kathleen K. Reardon. 'The Potential Role of Persuasion in Adolescent Aids Prevention', in R. Rice and C. Atkin, eds. *Public Communication Campaigns*, Newbury Park: Sage, 1989.

10.   William J. McGuire. 'Theoretical Foundations of Campaigns', in R. Rice and C. Atkin, eds. *Public Communication Campaigns*, Newbury Park: Sage, 1989.

11.   Arvind Singhal and Everett M. Rogers. 'Educating Through Television'. *Populi*, 16, 1, 1989.

12.   Todd Gitlin. 'Prime Time Ideology: The Hegemovie Process in Television Entertainment'. *Social Problems*, XXVI, February, 1979.

WRITING MESSAGE SPECIFICATIONS AND OBJECTIVES 9

Armed with information and advice from the audience and from experts, the production team is now ready to decide what community discussion and reflection it wants to stimulate. As the Cheshire Cat told Alice in Wonderland: *Where you* *ought to go from here depends on where you want to get to*. This chapter focuses on using audience lifestyle data and audience needs assessment to *outline the strategy* for the development message or series of messages. These outlines constitute the 'specifications' (specs) to which each writer-producer will conform, and by which each message will be evaluated. Subject specialists and audience researchers collaborate with the media producer to prepare the specs. They are a particularly valuable means of ensuring continuity when several writers and producers work on different parts of a series.

It is standard procedure to develop and follow exact specifications in the manufacture of such things as nuts, bolts, and screws. Products such as these must meet prescribed performance criteria. **Producers of development communication messages have tended to be casual about content and form specifications and how to meet them,** *because governments and grass roots organizations rarely measure the impact of messages on the audience. There is no attempt at accountability.* Two examples of media organizations that systematically prepare message specifications are the Children's Television Workshop in New York and the Development Education and Communication Unit of the Government of India's Space Technology Applications Centre in Ahmedabad, India.

The Children's Television Workshop prepares specifications for *Sesame Street* in the form of a **scriptwriter's manual**. The manual is prepared by subject specialists, audience researchers, and producers. Here, the production team will set guidelines using the best minds in the country as resources. They do not have to worry whether they omitted some crucial child development perspective, because they have the guidance of child development experts. Given the general goal of teaching *symbolic representation* to preschoolers, the specific objective for a program teaching children *word-matching* will state: 'Given a printed word, the child can select an identical printed word from a set of printed words'. Note the clarity. The producers know exactly what they are expected to achieve, and against what criteria they will be evaluated. Treatment and content recommendations in the manual tell the producers to try the following:

Use words with different numbers of letters which fail to match; compare two words letter by letter; ask viewers to find the different word when three identical words and a different word are

presented simultaneously; construct a letter-by-letter match from a large pool of letters; present words which matched in all senses except type face or capitalization.

Specifications for science education television programs were prepared by teams of scientists, science educators, and television producers at the Space Applications Centre (SAC) during the Satellite Instructional TV Experiment in the mid-1970s in India. The specifications consisted of 142 'briefs', one for each program. The general objective of the series was to have primary school students indicate that science was everywhere—in bicycles, in trees, and in village ponds, rather than being something that happened in laboratories far from their villages. The emphasis was on teaching the scientific method of analysis rather than on transferring scientific discoveries and facts. The following program specification is brief No. 2–2 entitled *Web of Life*, from the 1974 science education 'briefs'. This first attempt at writing specifications for media series

---

A Typical Specification Sheet from the Bombay Science Studio

Objectives: The child should be able to:
1. Understand that being human does not make us totally independent of everything else in our environment
2. Understand that human beings are just one species among scores of living creatures on earth

'Science' content:
1. The concept of ecosystem
2. Interdependence of all living organisms
3. Coexistence of plant and animal life

Application to the rural environment:
The total destruction of any one form of life may have dire consequences for life patterns on earth.
Example 1: Destruction of plant life has an effect on rainfall.
Example 2: Destruction of birds increases the insect population which destroys crops

Questions to ponder:
Does this earth *belong* to human beings only?

on the Indian subcontinent takes into account the audience's rural environment. Its approach to teaching and learning includes raising questions, thus requiring the viewer to be active rather than passive. No doubt, subsequent attempts at the preparation of specifications will have included statements as to how to measure the achievement of objectives. That element was missing in this first exercise.

Ideally, a message's specifications should embody comprehensive and final recommendations from content specialists and audience analysts as to focus and direction. These 'specs' are equivalent to the architect's blueprint or a teacher's lesson plans. Media production crews should not have to worry about the correctness of content and its audience sensitivity—the 'specs' should be their guide. Thus, specifications provide the terms of reference for the scriptwriter, set designer, and sound recorder. Specifications for all messages that contribute to the same overall goal should be completed before any production is envisaged. Such long-term planning for a topic ensures comprehensive conceptualization of the many steps required to reach the general objective (e.g., use of organic fertilizer). Thus, specifications plan for transitions between individual programs, continuity, and cumulative build-up. These are crucial for the achievement of specific goals, especially when different part-time writers may work on different parts of a series. What kinds of issues need to be clarified in the specifications? The following sections discuss each subheading of a typical specifications sheet.

Audience

Who are the primary beneficiaries of this message? What social, economic, political, and cultural background do they come from? What are their demographics, their psychographics? This section reminds the writer and artist about essential characteristics of their audience, to ensure that they pitch the message at the right level and feature culturally appropriate characters, dialogues, and settings.

General Objective of the Series

A statement of the general objective of the series indicates the common goal toward which all messages should be working. The production team specifies what the series should facilitate in the audience, in terms of knowledge gains, questioning, reflection, behavior modifications, and discussion. The objective of the science education series produced at the Indian Space Centre for use in primary schools was to teach children to use the scientific method to analyze their everyday environments. Psychologists, television producers, and audience researchers worked together to 'increase the motivation of 7- to 10-year old village children to improvise solutions to their work and play problems, rather than do nothing', in another television series produced at the Space Centre.

Typical Message Specifications Sheet

Audience:

General objective of series:

Specific measurable objectives for this message:

Mix of message delivery channels:

Content:

Media:

Other supportive media:

Treatment:

Infrastructure required in audience community for achievement of message objective:

Specific Measurable Objectives for this Message

Every production team needs to have a very clear, measurable objective: after exposure to this message, what is the audience supposed to know, feel, or do, under which conditions, and how well? This statement constitutes the criterion for evaluating the production team's performance. When clearly defined objectives are lacking, the production team has no sound basis for selecting content or form. It is also impossible to evaluate whether or not the message was communicated. A message in a series aimed at reducing deaths from infant diarrhea might have the following objective: after exposure to this message, 80 percent of mothers in the reproductive age group will be able to identify Litrosol as the oral rehydration therapy for infants in a chemist's store. The specifications writer should avoid sentences open to alternative interpretations; for instance, 'The audience will have a critical appreciation for....' This statement is not explicit enough until it indicates what the audience will be doing to demonstrate the desired critical appreciation so there can be no disagreement between evaluators.[1]

Mix of Message Delivery Channels

Public service agencies in agriculture, health, and education which commission media campaigns in support of their goals should know that the use of several media channels and multiple presentations in a variety of eye- and ear-catching formats is recommended. Very few messages will impact their audiences if only a single channel carries them. Each medium has limited strengths: some channels are good at introducing a subject, while others are better at giving reminders. Some media are good at presenting concrete details, while others are better at abstractions. Some media attract one kind of audience segment, while other channels have a completely different audience. The media mix will vary, depending on the message-audience combination in each case, and the available budget.

Content

In this section of the 'specs', the message design team analyzes the gap between the goal and present audience reality. The subject specialist's role is to advise the team on how to fill the gap between audience needs and overall objectives. Their decision is documented under this subheading. A general guideline is to limit the amount of 'content' that goes into any single message and to make sure the content is stated and detailed unambiguously. Audiences are generally busy doing other things in distracting situations when they happen upon this particular message.

Media

Under this heading, the production team specifies which medium this particular message will be designed for. At what times and places will the message be distributed? How often? With which other media will it be orchestrated? Are presentations in other media going to support this same content or must it stand along to succeed?

Treatment

With audience profile data in, the audience researcher and media producer are in a position to visualize the appropriate format and treatment for this topic. The questions are: what kind of message format will cause this message to capture and hold this audience's attention, promote audience comprehension, and ensure that the audience can identify with and emulate the performers and presenters? How should the content be treated to motivate this audience of reflect on the message? How should one stress the relevance of the content and the ease with which it may be implemented? What lexicon or vocabulary should be used with this audience on this topic, and what should be avoided? What should be the length, pace, and complexity of the message? The preceding chapter investigated this form and treatment decision. The next chapter describes how to confirm that the production team made the right decision.

Essential Infrastructure Required for Goal Achievement

Chapter 2 has stressed that it is futile to package information for the masses in appropriately small, digestible, attractive bites, when the majority do not have access to the inputs and infrastructure required to use the information. It is a common misconception that only information and education are needed to change attitudes and behaviors. Smokers frequently have all the facts about the damaging effects of smoke on their own lungs and on those of their family members. But, laws are required to restrict the settings in which smoking is allowed in order for media persuasion to work. A reduction in the incidence of drunken driving will require the institution of honest police roadblocks and jail sentences and the confiscation of driving licenses, in conjunction with appeals through the media. Farmers need the resources to adopt the agricultural innovations they hear about on the radio. If attitudes and behaviors do not change after concerted media campaigns, this does not mean the messages were poorly designed. It is conceivable that they were not comprehensively integrated with the infrastructure changes required for the achievement of goals. Successful communication is only one of the elements involved in effecting a change in behavior and values. Under this subheading, the production team documents how their media messages fit into the larger development context.

Chapters 7 and 8 focused on the need to study audience preferences as to the content and form of development communications messages before making any attempt at producing them. This chapter focused on how to organize preproduction audience advice into development communication specifications for the production team. The production team is now ready to experiment with the production of 'roughs' and prototype programs. The next chapter looks at audience responses to pilot programs and rough ideas. It will discuss how to determine whether or not audience preferences were interpreted correctly and how to modify form and content to be better suited to an audience.

Notes and References

1. A simple readable book in this area is by R.F. Mager. *Preparing Instructional Objectives*. Palo Alto, California: Fearon Publishers, 1975, second edition.

PRETESTING AUDIENCE RESPONSE 10

Bamboo poles were used in a program in Asia to demonstrate how condoms should be used. Months later, there were large numbers of pregnant women. Had the men not used the condoms? Yes, they had—they had put them on bamboo poles.[1]

A Caribbean script said, 'A breast-fed baby *rarely* gets diarrhoea'. Due to mispronunciation by the presenter, the message sounded like, 'A breast-fed baby *really* gets diarrhoea'. [2]

T he Asian and the Caribbean production teams could have visited their audiences to understand their lifestyles and values, consulted subject experts, written clear objectives and specifications, and still have produced these messages that the audience misunderstood. The reason is: once the information on audience-responsive topics and audience-responsive treatment is in, the team has to make decisions, e.g., will animation be better than live action? Will traditional cultural formats like puppet shows carry the message? Will two important points in a message rather than one constitute information overload? Will an audience of low-income rural mothers accept advice on child care from a glamorous film star? Hunches, educated guesses and uncertainty seem to dominate the message conceptualization and execution process.

This chapter is about midproduction testing of draft messages on their intended audience to help production teams to strengthen audience appeal, comprehension, credibility, and utility of their messages. That communication of nontrivial issues like employment, hunger, water, disease, justice, and equality should founder on seemingly trivial issues related to words, gestures, characters, sets, and actions is amazing but true. Should the graphic artist reduce the text and make the visuals speak louder in his/her poster? Should the filmmaker use a testimonial format, or a dramatic portrayal of a real life situation in a documentary? Should the radio producer use an older traditional authority figure, a modern authority figure, or audience peer? Should the message's appeal be emotional, logical, or humorous? The answers are specific to a particular time, place, and issue.

What Materials Can Be Pretested

Before generating new materials, production teams may want to test *existing messages* produced by others that deal with the content and audience assigned to them, to learn from the mistakes of other producers. Some producers then test semifinished rough versions of new messages, be they thirty- to fifty-word paragraphs describing a story, paste-ups, draft scripts or storyboards. Video producers design storyboards with line drawings (animatics) or photographs (photomatics) and then record them, frame by frame, with the camera zooming in or out and panning left to right to create motion, if a rough cut of a film or video production is required for pretesting. Television networks in the United States also use thirty- to fifty-word paragraphs describing a potential program or series and show them to convenient samples of passersby at shopping centers, as one of the many factors that go into deciding to produce a program. The same networks also finance a finished execution of a message as a pilot to enable testing of the approach for a series.

Who Should Conduct Audience Pretesting?

Ideally, an audience researcher familiar with the process of media production who knows the audience's culture and language is required. He/she must be an extrovert who can draw out responses from the audience by putting them at ease. He/she should be a good listener rather than a talker. Overriding all these requirements is that the selected person should not have a vested interest in defending the test message. Since the audience researcher who did the life-style profile and needs assessment that formed (or should have formed) the basis of the content and form of the pretest message is a co-producer of sorts, it would be preferable to request an audience researcher who was not involved in this production to actually conduct the pretests and summarize the findings in response to a list of questions that the message design team needs answered.

When the message design team is a one-person operation or a small unit, it is common for a community worker to be trained as a media producer. This multipurpose activist must follow the guidelines in this chapter carefully. Despite commitment to the Cause or the Community, media producers and researchers with ego invested in their productions frequently find excuses to ignore early warnings from pretest audiences rather than take precautions that will save their organization time, money, and effort.

On Whom

Frequently, the difference in the production cost of a message that communicates with its audience as against one that does not is very small. This is because of the tendency to equate production values with audience impact when this is not necessarily so. The power structure is such that ministries of education, health, and agriculture usually decide whether a message is appropriate. While they are in a position to determine technical accuracy of content, its communication ability should be determined by audience testing. An audience researcher typically pretests selected messages by obtaining reactions from small samples of audience members. Audience pretesting of presentations is critical because the subject expert and producer designing the message and the audience receiving the message frequently live in different economic, political, social, and cultural worlds. The message designers and the message receivers are *heterophilous*. Even if producers were born in the same neighborhoods and went to the same schools and places of worship as their audiences, their training and competence in a new language—the language of graphic art or audio or video or film—sets them apart from their audiences who have learned the language of the medium as consumers. Naturally, those audiences with low media exposure follow the media language less well. This includes audiences of a newly introduced medium in a region, and audiences of mobile film teams who normally do not have access to films.

How many audience members should be interviewed in a pretest? Twenty-five to thirty-five randomly selected members of a distinct segment in the intended audience should suffice. Review Chapter 6 before reading further.

What Questions to Ask

What would a production team want to know about the appropriateness of its form and content? What questions on communicability can audience pretesting of a message answer for a production team? Pretesting can indicate the following:

Attention-Getting and Attention-Holding Appeal

No matter how simple and clear a message might be, it will be lost unless it grabs audience attention and holds it. While a sensational gimmick at the start of a message may be a great attention-getter, it may not hold audience attention throughout. The production team needs to include appeals that hope to do both, and to then check with a small sample of the audience on what attention levels the draft messages achieved before going ahead with final production.

Audience segmentation is crucial for determining which appeal will work for which group. Appeals that work in one setting may not work in another. An appeal that asks an audience member to be pioneering (e.g., 'be the first person in your village to...') may be appropriate for political and economic elites with high religious status. A village power structure may penalize a pioneering, forward-looking initiative by a person of low socioeconomic status and his/her peers may consider the action presumptuous. Colors symbolize different feelings in different cultures.

> To ensure that mothers understood the growth monitoring charts used on their infants, a project in Ecuador decided to color-code the normal-to-malnourished range based on community perceptions. The project gave pictures of three children—healthy, sick, and very sick—to mothers, and asked them to match them with a range of colors. Instead of red being the danger zone as in the cities of the world, the mothers chose red as the sign of a healthy child (because red cheeks were associated with well-being). Yellow or light pink was chosen to signify the loss of skin tone and illness, and white (or green) was chosen to signify the very sick child.[3]

Designing a single communication series for the *average* audience member implies lower production costs than several series on the same topic for different audiences—but it has only a limited impact on everybody. To have a significant impact, the producer has to tailor appeals to coherent homogenous groups.

Comprehension and Immediate Recall

An audience that pays careful attention to a glitzy message does not necessarily understand what the message is trying to communicate. Perfect communication is a very rare occurrence. A certain proportion of miscomprehension may simply reflect a natural error rate associated with one-way communication in general. Audience members bring their past experiences and their present expectations to each communication transaction and may interpret or misinterpret communication in terms of their previous experiences. Miscomprehension due to individual past experiences or the current mental set may well be impossible to eliminate entirely. Whether the audience understands the production teams's use of the language of the medium will determine comprehension of the message. The different life and language experiences of producers and audiences may cause them to interpret the plot, characters, settings, timing, sequencing, music, camera angles, lighting, slow motion, pixilation, and speech balloons quite differently from each other. A poster promoting the use of 'condoms' among Australian aboriginals was perceived as promoting the fruit of the local *quandong* tree. The modified poster was revised to incorporate the local terminology for condoms: 'frenchies'. Audience pretesting of roughs can tell the production crew whether their educated guesses will work before they spend a lot of money and time to produce a final version of their message.

Many urban mass media producers and subject experts feel that the reasons for miscomprehension of their development communications lie in the illiteracy of their rural audiences. It would be instructive for them to read the findings of the American Association of Advertising Agencies[4] study of the comprehension and miscomprehension of television and print ads in the United States. This study used sixty test commercials. Each and every television communication showed miscomprehension at least some of the time by some of the viewers. Viewers miscomprehended about 30 percent of the core informational content contained within each communication. No single group was highest on miscomprehension of television ads: it seemed to occur in all age, income and education levels to virtually the same degree. In Asia, Africa, Latin America, and the Caribbean, the level of familiarity with the language of the medium might also be expected to make a difference. A follow-up study of magazine communication in the United States conducted by the same team found that almost everyone miscomprehended some part of what they read. Readers miscomprehended about 21 percent of the meanings contained in the typical magazine article with an additional average 'don't know' rate of 16 percent. The difference between televised content and print content is that formal education and income *are* significantly related to miscomprehension of print. *The root of the miscomprehension problem seems to be the natural human tendency to make inferences.* Audiences exposed to communications make inferences regarding the topic which they then believe to be true and to have been explicitly stated (when it was not).

Pretesting helps identify possible reasons for miscomprehension, and helps remove these threats to comprehension. It does not predict how much knowledge gain will take place.

Utility

The personal relevance of media content to the audience member will determine its usefulness, irrespective of its style. Why should typical audience members bother with messages that are irrelevant to their problems and interests, inappropriate to their culture, and too capital-intensive for their limited resources to be able to support?

Credibility

Does the style of presentation make the content appear trustworthy, reliable, and believable? Do the sources of information used in the message appear honest? Does the information sound correct in the context of local beliefs the audience lives with? This is centrally related to acceptance of the message content.

Most production teams would welcome an early warning of problems related to attention, comprehension, utility, and credibility. A message design team can ask specific additional questions depending on what they need to know before plunging into final production.

How to Collect Audience Reactions

The production team wants to know if its message design will get and hold attention, be comprehended, believed, and acted on. Chapter 6 on audience research methods describes how to get answers to these questions. For program tryouts, be sure to select audience members who represent your audience. Use an objective impersonal mechanical process to select typical audience members to ensure against bias. Use a combination of information collection methods, e.g., observation followed by group interviews and individual interviews.

The easiest, most frequently used procedure for audience testing of audio programs, video cassettes, films, and personal reading material involves getting together a *focus group* of eight to ten audience members, showing them the test material unobtrusively along with two to three other messages, watching their reactions to the test message, and then asking them specific questions focused on its content and form. When the researcher is testing a poster, she/he should exhibit it among other posters where the audience will see it. She/he would then get an idea of its attention-getting ability. Passersby who stop to look at it could be asked questions, in addition to pretesting through focus groups.

The researcher should first ask questions of pretest audiences that start with their general impressions of the several messages they were presented. Rather than putting words in the mouth of audiences by asking leading questions such as 'You liked the program, didn't you', it is better to ask open-ended questions that allow the audience to speak at length in their own words. Then proceed to probing questions about particular messages, and particular parts of messages the team has doubts about. The team might want reactions to the title used, the names of characters, the color of costumes, the settings, words, music, pictorial technique, camera movements and editing styles. If the audience failed to spontaneously comment on a crucial part of the message, they might be asked to review the material a second time. The researcher might then ask if the pretest group noticed anything this time that they missed before. If no answer is forthcoming, she/he may point to the particular item and ask the audience what it means to them. This will tell the producer why this element was ignored, and how it could be modified.

Pretesting Condom Communications

One African country designed alternative formulations to arrive at the final form of television spots encouraging condom use as protection against AIDS. The intended audience was initially thought to be sexually active men. Initial pretests indicated that this audience was not homogenous: in addition to age, economic class, occupation, and rural-urban differences, those who had experience of sexually transmitted diseases were easier to convince than those who did not. Therefore, the production team designed different messages for two different segments within this audience: young male patients at sexually transmitted disease clinics, and the general population.

The content focused on why condoms should be used to prevent AIDS. The production team used different presenters to test if the information was more credible if it came from a physician versus a peer. To save money, the production team used slides with accompanying audio tapes to pretest the difference. Both segments preferred their peers as presenters. The pretest group felt the doctor was 'preachy'. They preferred positive images of 'safe', sexually active couples over negative images of AIDS patients, vernacular phrases over medically correct terminology, and realistic portrayals over dramatic exaggerated presentations.[5]

Procedure

A standard pretest information collection procedure follows.

1. Observation During Pretest Exposure

Let exposure to the puppet show, audio, video, or print material take place in as natural and usual a setting as possible. If the researcher is testing a poster, display it *with other posters* in a location similar to where it would be posted after final production and distribution. If audiences will view the radio and television programs under production in the kitchen while meals are being prepared and children are demanding attention, or in a central location where the community gathers, make sure the researcher presents the tape in similar settings rather than in sterile alien studios. The team should always ensure that test messages are presented between two or three other materials designed for the same audience to avoid alerting the audience to which message is being tested, and thus biasing their responses.

Attention-getting:
The researcher should look for indications of the attention-getting potential of the message such as the following: did passersby stop and look at the poster you are testing? Did the cover of the printed pamphlet cause the audience member's expression to change? Did he/she make any exclamations? When the audio or audiovisual (film, television, slide-tape show) started, what was the expression on the viewer/listener's face?

Attention-holding:
A good message designer recognizes that merely getting the attention of the audience initially is not enough. The researcher should also look for the following indications of attention-holding throughout exposure to the message: did the audience member watch/listen to/read the *whole* message diligently? When was she/he distracted or bored?

2. Questions to Ask After Exposure

The researcher should not interrupt *first* exposure to a puppet show, radio program, television program, or poster with questions. Wait until the pretest audience has finished reading, listening, and watching. Ask the following questions about audience reactions to the whole program (holistic testing), and *then* probe reactions to specific parts (atomistic testing). It is important to probe, pause, and *listen*. The audience's voice is more important than the researcher's.

General reaction to the whole message:
The following are illustrations of questions that should be asked in the respectful form of the local language: what did you think about the poster/pamphlet/program/show you just saw/heard? (Probe: Anything else?)

Was there anything you liked about the poster/program? What was it? (Probe: e.g., Characters? Music? Dialogue? Illustrations?) Was there anything you disliked about it? If yes, what was it you disliked? (Probe)

Was there anything that your friends and family would be offended by? What is offensive? Why is it offensive?

Comprehension of main idea:
The researcher should constantly try to be unbiased. Questions

should be phrased in an open-ended fashion so the audience knows criticism and praise are equally useful. Illustrations follow: What was the main idea that the (specify poster, radio program) was trying to get across? What else? Anything else?

Does the (specify program/poster, etc.) want you to do anything in particular? (Wait for answer and then probe:) What does the poster/program/pamphlet want you to do? Will you do it? Why? Why not?

Was the message easy to understand or hard to follow? Was there anything confusing about this message? What was confusing? Were there any parts (words, songs, action) that your friends would have a difficult time understanding? Please name them. What do these words mean: (read one word at a time from a list of crucial words used in the program/poster and write down the exact answers the audience gives)

Credibility:

Did you believe the information presented in the message? Was there anything you did not believe? What was it? Did you trust the expertise of the characters who were presenting the information (name program characters one at a time and pause for answer) in the message? Why/why not?

Utility:

For what kind of person would this message be most useful? Was there anything in the program that would be useful for someone like you?

Did you learn anything new from this message? What did you learn?

What information would you have liked the program/poster to give you?

General suggestions:

Do you have any suggestions you would like to make to the team who produced the poster/program on how to improve it?

Whether the procedure described—observation of pretest audience exposure to the test message followed by interviewing—is conducted individually or in groups or both depends on the medium, the audience, and time-money budgets. The researcher could consider the proportion of individual passersby who stop and the length of time they pause could be the measure of attention-getting and attention-holding, if the pretest poster was displayed in the community for whom it is designed. Some of those who stop may be willing to submit to five-minute individual interviews. After display of draft messages and observation of exposure, the researcher should conduct interviews with some individuals and groups, taking care to include only members of the intended audience. This combination of observation, and individual and group interviews with representative members of audience chosen in some random fashion will provide the production team with a wealth of information.

UNICEF Pretesting Experiences

George McBean, Ane Haaland, and Sylvie Cohen, who have been/are with UNICEF, have produced useful guidelines for communications designers from their pretesting experiences. The following are perennial favorites from Haaland's work in Nepal:[6]

Graphic artists frequently draw a 'bubble' over a person's head to let literate audiences know what the illustrated character is thinking or saying. Newly literate Nepalese villagers could read the text but were not familiar with the bubble as a graphic convention. They thought this symbol was a garlic pod.

Media producers and pediatricians are often urban dwellers while development communication audiences are frequently rural. It was, therefore, natural for an urban pediatrician and artist to show a rural-looking mother using an urban artifact (a teaspoon) in a poster highlighting proper infant-feeding practices. Not surprisingly, pretest audiences wondered whether the poster was urging them to buy teaspoons and to abandon the traditional practice of the village mother who feeds her child with her fingers. An incidental aspect that did not fit into the local culture thus became the center of attention.

Symbols from Western graphic conventions such as the skull and crossbones, check marks ($\vee$), and crosses (X) used by urban-based artists in Nepal were also not understood by new literates in rural areas. If usable alternative rural symbols understood over large areas do not exist, George McBean (now in UNICEF, Barbados) suggests *teaching* the meaning of new symbols before using them.

Using Pretest Data

Building pretesting into the process of message design in media production requires time, effort, and resources. Grass roots organizations that use mass media as aids to community organization, self-development, and self-management are motivated to ensure the communicability of their messages. Large media production departments in government organizations see media production as their goal—whether their product communicates or not after it leaves their studios is frequently irrelevant as long as the boss and the minister like it. Audience research activities in such units rarely contribute to preproduction and midproduction decisions. When they do, what should the production team do with pretest findings? What should the media producer and audience researcher in the grass roots organization do?

If attention is low, change the format. If samples do not understand the scriptwriter's words and phrases, replace them with their own words. If the major point of the message is not grasped, remove the clutter, simplify the story, take out unnecessary characters, dialogues, scenes, and illustrations. Find different ways of reinforcing one central point. If the message is low on credibility, check what is wrong with the content before changing the presenter. If the sample does not think the information is useful, talk to the subject expert: check what the audience indicated its needs were, and see if the message can respond to them better.

How a Format for a Local News Program was Selected

In 1980, the Jamaica Broadcasting Corporation's new radio station in Central Jamaica was eager to design its local news program such that it was high on attention, comprehension, utility, and credibility. Audience lifestyle and values data indicated the need to explain the news in the locally spoken form of Jamaican English. What was also clear was that few audience members expected a station that was part of a network run out of the Prime Minister's office to tell the truth. What were the options for the production team?

The first decision was to present news and publicize events from the station's coverage area brought in by local residents and local agencies only. The next action involved the generation of three alternative program formats: straight reading of the news in British English as headquarters and the Western/ urban-oriented producers wanted, a reading of the news in the local *patois*, and a straight reading of the headlines in British English followed by a dramatized discussion of selected items by three villagers who met at the bus stop every evening to understand what the day's happenings meant for them. Producers designed three alternative formats for the same content. Researchers tested them by playing back audio cassettes in the villages surrounding the radio transmitter. Four villages in two distinct geographical-cultural regions of the coverage area were sampled; all available residents were interviewed as they were found, in groups or individually. The researcher followed the observation-and-interview procedure presented earlier in this chapter. The majority of the tested listeners in all age, occupation, sex, and cultural-geographic audience segments preferred the dramatic discussion-in-the-patois version of the news.[7]

How Do Industrially Advanced Countries Conduct Pretests?

The technology used in pretesting will depend on the availability of resources, and how serious the organization is about ensuring that meaning is shared between sender and receiver. The Children's Television Workshop in New York designed a science education series entitled *3-2-1 Contact* for 8- to 12-year olds. Researchers used several different methods of testing *existing* science films and television shows and two sets of five specially designed *test* shows. The purpose was to assess the appeal (boring/interesting) of each segment, the appeal of characters (the cast) in the program, the comprehension of each segment, and the utility of the program for home viewing and school viewing.[8]

During exposure to a program, children indicated whether a segment was boring or interesting every ten seconds. Each child indicated his/her choice by pressing a key on his/her wireless, a battery-powered hand unit resembling a calculator. The child used the same keypad to respond to questions about favorite segments and characters. At the end of each session, researchers collected the hand units and transferred the data to a microcomputer and diskette for analysis and storage. This Program Evaluation and Analysis Computer system does away with the need to write responses or have individual interviewers per viewer. Another advantage is that results are available in fifteen minutes after data collection for display in colorful formats on a television monitor. Producers can simultaneously view each ten-second program segment on one screen and the audience's interesting/boring response to it on another.

Additional methods of testing appeal included segment voting and triplet voting. Segment voting required viewers to choose the best and least liked segments after viewing them. This final retrospective judgement is useful in cases where different segments have received similar responses on the program analyzer. Children were also asked to select the most and least liked segment from among a set of three (triplet) one-minute excerpts showing different topics.

Small group interviews, the freeze-frame technique, and children's re-narrations tested the comprehension of program messages. In small group interviews, a researcher used a common set of prepared questions to probe in-depth perceptions of program material with three or four children per group. When researchers find comprehension of a particular event or segment is in question, they freeze the frame on the screen to probe what has happened in the story so far. Children who have viewed the program once provide the narration on the second viewing when the sound is turned off, to check comprehension of the whole program and the establishment of transitions between segments.

What is impressive about the testing of this series is the meticulous attention paid to detail exemplified by the many different ways of checking on both comprehension and appeal before finalizing what a series is going to contain. The US commercial television networks present a contrast in how they test their entertainment series. The primary goal is attention-getting and attention-holding in order that maximum audiences will be exposed to the advertising; the larger the audiences, the higher the advertising rates for the particular program slot, and hence the higher the revenues of the broadcasting company.

The CBS (Columbia Broadcasting System) in the United States makes decisions on the production of approximately 80 percent of all series *after* pilot testing. Tests use questionnaires, focus group discussions, and electrical signals from buttons. CBS invites approximately 100 tourists visiting New York to watch a program or a pilot for a series. Depressing red and green buttons on their seats at CBS indicates their positive and negative reactions as they watch the program. Questionnaires distributed after the program contain closed-ended and open-ended questions that compare the test program to other successful programs and investigate reactions to the setting and characters. Responses are segmented according to age and education. CBS acknowledges the weakness of its audience testing: unusual and pioneering shows which may actually get high viewership when transmitted may get low scores during tests because they are different from the sample's expectation of what is socially desirable.

The American Broadcasting Corporation (ASC) contracts the bulk of its testing to the privately-owned Audience Studies Incorporated (ASI). ASI's theaters test titles, concepts, stars, pilots, and continuations of series quickly and cheaply—each seat has a five-position switch (very dull, dull, fair, good, and very good) for audience response. Questionnaires are also distributed after viewing to investigate demographic facts (e.g., age, income), lifestyle, and consumption factors. While ASI recruits test audiences from the streets, through the mail and through telephone calls, it analyzes only the reponses of those viewers who match the program's intended audience profile.

The National Broadcasting Service has ASI rent unused cable channels to test its programs in homes. It invites about 125 cable subscribers across the country by telephone the night before to watch the test program. An interviewer telephones after the program is over to investigate responses. Audience reactions are classified according to age and income segments.

Clearly, US networks see the importance of pretesting programs. However, the methods they use to select their samples and elicit audience responses leave a lot to be desired, particularly when compared with the care exercised by the Children's Television Workshop as demonstrated in science education programs presented here.

Early Warning System

Media producers should conceive of pretesting (of ideas, concepts, titles, characters, settings, and message drafts) on small samples as an opportunity to diagnose problems, not as a predictor of success. It is a rough-and-ready diagnostic to give the production team an early warning on attention, comprehension, utility, and credibility while revisions are still possible and affordable.

Since pretests are usually low-cost attempts at getting insightful responses from a small sample of the larger audience, they cannot provide quantitative guarantees. For example, they cannot state that Version A will get 10 percent higher comprehension scores than Version B. Media producers should not make predictions about broad-scale results in the total audience from small sample interviews. Pretests of greater precision are possible but they require greater investments of time and money that relatively well-endowed production systems are unwilling to spend or are uable to. Many production teams feel that the combination of early warnings from small group testing with their own experience and judgement suffice.

Small group testing requires extra caution: caution in selecting a sample representative of the whole audience, and caution in designing questions and interpreting results without bias. Production teams who do their own testing will naturally be tempted to select friendly samples and phrase questions that will show appreciation of their hunches and hard work. Biased selection of samples and questionnaire design can easily guarantee support for the production team in the formative stages. However, in the final analysis, after the program is transmitted, the audience will decide. Production teams who want an early indication of whether the audience will find their communication attempts comprehensible, attention-getting, attention-holding, useful, and credible will ensure they keep their biases out of pretesting design.

Some Limitations

Pretesting of appeal and comprehension does not provide any indication of whether the program will promote gains in knowledge or changes in feelings and behavior. This is dependent on selection of audience-responsive topics as outlined in Chapter 7. Nor can a researcher who conducts an unbiased pretest with representative samples in a natural exposure setting, and interprets sample responses on attention, comprehension, utility, and credibility with care, be guaranteed a final production that automatically rates high on appeal and comprehensibility. This will depend on how responsive the production team is to pretest findings. A script idea that tests well can be rendered ineffective by poor casting, inappropriate sets, bad lighting, and the like. Pretesting is like a red-orange-green traffic light: of itself, it does not guarantee that the motorist (or the production team) will respond to it.

After several pretests, the production team may feel its content and treatment are right for the audience. The formative stages are over. The message goes into final production and is distributed to audiences.

MONITORING THE PROCESS

Many production teams and project managers want to ensure that the media plan (selection of particular channels) is appropriate for the intended audience. Given how intensive audience-responsive production has been, researchers want to ensure that the intended audience was actually exposed to the message. Regular (monthly, weekly) panels of media audiences are used to obtain audience ratings in some countries. A randomly selected representative sample of the audience maintains diaries of their broadcast listening and viewing or have meters attached to their sets that record the channel and the time it is turned on in industrially advanced countries. During the Satellite Instructional Television Experiment in India in the mid-1970s, participant observers of the community viewing situation were located in each of a panel of randomly selected villages across the country. The researcher observed audience composition and attention and also conducted interviews with a small sample of the viewers to check on postprogram comprehension, utility, and credibility. Individual production teams received computerized results.

EVALUATING THE IMPACT

After message reception, the hardworking production team deserves to know:

1. How many audience members saw/heard the message? **Did it communicate?** Did the audience understand it, consider it useful and believe it?
2. **Did the message reach its development goals?** Did the message cause the audience to question, reflect, discuss, and plan their own development as stated in the specific measurable objectives?

This is report card time. How to answer monitoing and impact evaluation questions is the topic of other books that deal with **summative research**—a summation of audience effects compared with message goals. The audience is the final judge of whether the production team made the right decisions. Awards and praise from colleagues, bosses, and friends tell the production team whether their messages worked with their colleagues, bosses, and friends. Summative evaluators use special, large sample surveys and in-depth studies to test whether the message reached its goals (e.g., in agriculture, health, or community organization), even if message comprehension was high. Separate studies of impact are necessary for the production team to know whether their messages worked with their audiences. Such data should be used to design the goals, content, and form of *future* messages.

The next chapter is a summary of the argument and methodology presented in this book.

Notes and References

1. *UNICEF News*, issue 114, 4, 1982, p. 10.
2. Ibid.
3. Marcia Griffiths. 'Growth Monitoring and Nutrition Education' in USAID, *Nutrition Education and Social Marketing Field Support*. Washington, DC: USAID Project 936–5113, July 1987.
4. Jacob Jacoby and Wayne D. Joyer. *The Miscomprehension and Comprehension of Print Communication*. Hillsdale, NJ: Lawrence Erlbaum, 1987.
5. World Health Organization Global Program on AIDS Health Promotion Division. *Guide for Planning: Annex 1 on Pretesting* (draft), 1989. This is modified and adapted from the hypothetical example presented.

6.   Ane Haaland. *Pretesting Communication Materials: A Manual for Trainers and Supervisors*. UNICEF, 1984.

7.   Bella Mody. 'Resourcing the Audience: A Folk Tale From Jamaica'. *Gazette*, 38, 1986, pp. 147–60.

8.   Milton Chen. 'Television, Science and Children: Formative Evaluation for 3–2–1 Contact'. *Educational Technology Systems*, 9, 3, 1980–81.

The thesis of this book is that mass media support for community participation-based national transformation requires audience-based message design to succeed. The book therefore specifies how to involve the audience in the selection of the content and form of development communication messages so these messages (*a*) actually communicate with their intended audiences (*b*) in support of national transformation in countries of the South. Authoritarian, top-down instructions from the ruling elites to the masses generate compliance (if that), not participation. Only a participatory process can lead to a participatory system. Hence, an audience participation-based approach is recommended for message design (means), in support of national transformation into a self-sustaining, participatory community decision making system (end).

The media producer designs messages in response to the vision of national development of the governmental, intergovernmental, or nongovernmental agency which finances her/his work. Chapter 1 briefly reviews the dominant path to national development that continues to prevail, and then explains the parallel history of the mass media's usage. National development has been conceptualized as an economic growth process that can be accelerated by the use of technology. Cultural, political, psychological, and spiritual aspects of national transformation have received little or no attention under this framework. Development plans have been divided into sectors to match governmental department bureaucracies. The focus of attention has been on the symptoms (e.g., hunger, malnutrition) of underdevelopment rather than the root structural causes that perpetuate the problem, e.g., inequality based on class, race, gender, state and transnational corporations. Development plans have been symptomatic treatments rather than attempts to attack the causes. Without radical structural change, the symptoms have continued to appear and the same so-called development plans have perpetuated themselves as continuously needed treatments. The conceptualization of the 1970s requires mass participation in decision making on the root causes of the problem and implications of alternative solutions in the spirit of grass roots democracy: the people decide how to meet their local and national needs in an ecologically responsible mode that learns from other nations and their own history, but blindly imitates none. The end and the means are the same: mass participation in decision making towards a self-sustaining system of mass participation in decision making. The specific paths chosen by individual nations will be varied.

The typical Third World state cannot be expected to initiate such broad-based participation, given that it is run by and in the interests of local capital, multinational capital, and the civil service bureaucracy. Action in favor of the marginal majority will have to come from those nongovernmental organizations which have a vested interest in the common (hu)man. A solidarity network of grass roots organizations is needed that will constitute an implacable lobby for the disenfranchised.

Chapter 1 shows how and why the economic growth and modernization model, with its matching top-down and West-to-East information transfer model, stood indicted in the mid-1970s. Events and forces that led to the indictment are documented so history is not ignored when planning anew. The role of US academics, a US-dominated UNESCO, and a well-intentioned USAID were central in identifying the mass media as potential public service agents in the 1960s. Like the carpenter equipped with a hammer who sees everything in the shape of nails, communication researchers and practitioners staked out major roles for themselves in the development 'business'. Elites and entrepreneurs in the recently independent nations of Asia and Africa were more interested in imitating Western Europe and America's use of the mass media for entertainment, financed by advertising. Given these diverse forces, the result was politically centralized imported media technology to carry wisdom from foreign and domestic centers of knowledge to the supposedly less knowledgeable poor. The structural biases (race, class, gender) imbedded in the information were ignored. The consequences of establishing a global monoculture that would destroy cultural and biological diversity are not fully understood even today. It should not have needed so many researchers to point out that like economic growth, information was trickling down these new pipelines slowly, and was generally acted on by those with more education, income, and property. No change in the structure of power and privilege was planned. Information flowed to the haves and perpetuated development gaps, rather then changed them.

In the 1970s, it was realized that planning of national development by the elite would naturally preserve the privileges of the elite while allowing only a trickle downwards. If the majority was allowed to participate in their own development, the results would be different. Horizontal information flows between people and between communities would have to be initiated by nongovernmental organizations, equipped with low-cost, portable media technologies where necessary, to develop a grass roots consensus on what kind of national development was wanted, and how to go about getting it. The participatory process would have to include everyone—property owners and the bureaucracy—if it had to be morally and ethically superior to the interest group conflicts of the past that continue into the 1990s. Nongovernmental organizations might want to consider systematic audience research for media message design as a means to expedite realization of the participatory approach to grass roots self-management of national development (that is now at least fifteen years old in 1991).

Chapter 2 presents the case for making the 'invisible audience' at the end of an information channel 'visible' to the media production team. If two people cannot communicate perfectly when talking face-to-face, why should one expect radio producers and graphic artists to communicate effectively with communities or individuals they cannot see or hear? Production teams must question the status of the long-distance magician that media channels were assigned in the 1960s. With little attention paid to technical accuracy of content and even less time spent on finding out what content intended audience members of a community need, the assumption has been that media messages will make a difference. Sometimes, the need may be for information on how to make better use of existing resources. In other cases, the need may be for information on how to get additional resources. The recommended approach is for the media production team to approximate the dialogue that enables communication in face-to-face interactions *before* going to their drawing boards and studios to design development communications. In simple terms, the recommendation is to *observe and listen before talking at communities* through one-way media.

Chapter 3 presents the idea of systematic involvement of samples of intended audiences in preproduction and midproduction message design to counteract the physical separation between sender and receiver in one-way mass media flows. This *audience first* approach makes the community the sender or source of development communications designed to meet their needs, thereby reorganizing the one-way monologue into a circular dialogue. The purpose of beginning with the audience is to find out what they need to know, and how the media should present this information in order that the audience will understand, believe, reflect, discuss, and act on the messages. The chapter presents systematic steps in audience research for mass media message design. It urges a sequence of at least two audience trips during the preparatory stages of an information campaign: the first to establish what to say and how to say it; the second to audience-test alternative formulations of development communication messages that the team has developed in response to their first visit. This approach is called *formative evaluation*.

Chapter 4 deals with how to implement the participatory *ideal*. It then questions the ethics of this supposed ideal and highlights the implementation problems encountered in Jamaica and India through case studies. It spells out the role of different members of a team in implementing audience-based formative evaluation. Ethical issues are: is the audience-based approach primarily *sophisticated* systematic manipulation? Is audience responsiveness only a means to achieve the state or the advertiser's ends?

Chapter 5 reviews what major researchers say on the effects of one-way media, and how to make the best of them. It describes the factors that influence the design of information programs, followed by specifications of likely audience outputs.

Chapters 6 to 10 are basic how-to-do-it chapters for those responsible for implementing participation in self-management of national transformation. Unfortunately, the genius of the well-intentioned ideologue of egalitarian community-based national development tends to be bored by implementation details. Some expect new relationships to emerge and sustain themselves spontaneously, given the wisdom of the new (fifteen-year old) approach. Others dismiss technology and systematic planning as unholy and tainted, given their utilization by the state and private capital. Builders know dreams do not become reality in a day. Politically correct visionary castles remain in the air without blueprints, work plans and deadlines. The task is massive and requires several disciplines. These chapters help media producers to give life to the participatory vision of national transformation.

Chapter 6 applies basic social science data collection methodologies to audience research for preproduction and midproduction message design. The presentation is designed for communication practitioners. Information collection guidelines stress the importance of listening to *representative* members of all audience segments, avoiding bias in selecting communities/individuals and phrasing questions to them, triangulating (combining) data collection

methods, and finally, being practical about what is possible to do given time and budget constraints. The major part of the chapter introduces the reader to a practical sequence of audience information collection activities.

Chapter 7 focuses on how to find out what the audience's needs are under different real-world development communication scenarios. It points out that needs assessment initiatives will differ, based on whether it is a development agency or a media agency initiating the inquiry, and whether it is a commercial outlet or a nonprofit unit. The chapter explains how to use the data to *select content* for development communication message design.

Chapter 8 applies audience research methods to decision making on *form* or presentation: which media will reach the intended audience, and which persuasive strategies and creative formats will be effective. This chapter describes an audience lifestyle profile—what information to collect, how to collect it, and in what form to present it to media producers. Once the data is in, the production team can make decisions on audience *segments*, and how to communicate with each. It stresses the need for a creative strategy that dispels the notion of boring, repetitive development communication followed by presenting examples of a range of media, modes, and appeals that could be explored.

Chapter 9 describes how to use audience data to draw up a strategy statement or *specifications* for each message *before* designing development communications messages. It provides an illustrative format that requires the technical expert, the production crew, and the audience researchers (if they are separate individuals) to get together and agree on the intended audience, the media, the content, the format of the content, the other messages and other media that would reinforce this message (or not), and the infrastructure that exists on the ground (or not) to enable utilization of the information presented. It includes examples of 'specifications'

Chapter 10 describes how to check whether or not the decisions made on the basis of audience data were correct interpretations of audience preferences. *Draft* messages are designed and tried out on samples of audience segments to verify their appeal, comprehension, credibility, and utility. It spells out the methodology and procedure of *pretesting*—what materials to pretest, on whom, what questions to ask, how to collect audience reactions. It also presents illustrative cases of the use of such an early warning system.

This chapter is the summary. What are the implications of this approach? Will it have any adopters? The implementation of this audience participation-based developed communication method depends on whether the media production team is actually charged with (*i*) *communication* (*ii*) to *promote participation* in national

transformation. Media production agencies in government and nongovernmental organizations must be informed of these twin performance criteria, retrained, and then evaluated by independent researchers on these criteria. The approach has been spelled out in simple step-by-step terms for ease of use by development workers and media producers without any social research training. Utilization of this approach requires scheduling *time for audience visits* in the production schedule. Since development of a nation is a long term community-based process, budgeting time for audience input into the design of messages that will facilitate reflection, community discussion, and action is fundamental. Media production systems that are in such a hurry to send their productions to the printer and the transmitter that they have no time for audience inputs in pre-production and midproduction are working to indulge themselves, rather than to facilitate national transformation. They are message design systems for the sake of *media production*, not for *development-support communication*. In development communication, the community audience is the client, the media and media staff are at their service.

APPENDIX

Selected Bibliography on Mass Media and National Development

This is a short reading list for interested readers who are beginning to read on this topic. To ensure availability in Third World settings, this selection is restricted to major books.

1. Emile G. McAnany. *Communication in the Rural Third World: The Role of Information in Development.* New York: Praeger, 1980.
2. Emile G. McAnany et al. *Communication and Social Structure: Critical Studies in Mass Media Research.* New York: Praeger, 1981.
3. Goodwin Chu and Wilbur Schramm. *Learning From Television: What the Research Says.* Washington, DC: National Association of Educational Broadcasters, 1979, fourth edition.

4. Juan E. Diaz Bordenave. *Communication and Rural Development*. Paris: UNESCO, 1977.

5. Cees Hamelink. *Cultural Autonomy in Global Communication*. New York: Longman, 1983.

6. Paul Hartman, B.R. Patil, and Anita Dighe. *The Mass Media and Village Life: An Indian Study*. New Delhi: Sage, 1989.

7. Goran Hedebro. *Communication and Social Change in Developing Countries: A Critical View*. Ames, Iowa: Iowa State University Press, 1980.

8. Robert C. Hornik. *Development Communication: Information, Agriculture and Nutrition in the Third World*. New York: Longman 1988.

9. Dean T. Jamison and Emile G. McAnany. *Radio for Education and Development*. Beverly Hills: Sage, 1978.

10. Neville Jayaweera *et al.*, eds. *Rethinking Development Communication*. Singapore: AMIC, 1987.

11. Meheroo Jussawalla and Donald M. Lamberton. *Communication, Economics and Development*. New York: Pergamon, 1982.

12. Elihu Katz and George Wedell. *Broadcasting in the Third World*. Cambridge, MA: Harvard University Press, 1977.

13. Daniel Lerner. *The Passing of Traditional Society*. Glencoe, Il: The Free Press, 1958.

14. Nkwabi Ng'wanakilala. *Mass Communication and Development of Socialism in Tanzania*. Dar es Salaam: Tanzania Publishing House, 1981.

15. Karle Nordeusheng and Herbert I. Schiller. *National Sovereignty and International Communication*. New York: Ablext, 1979.

16. Everett M. Rogers. *Communication and Development: Critical Perspectives*. Beverly Hills: Sage, 1982.

17. Prodipto Roy and others. *The Impact of Communication on Rural Development: An Investigation in Costa Rica and India*. Paris: UNESCO, 1969.

18. Herbert I. Schiller. *Communication and Cultural Domination*. New York: Partheon Books, 1976.

19. Wilbur Schramm. *Mass Media and National Development*. California: Stanford University Press, 1964.

20. Wilbur Schramm. *Big Media, Little Media*. Beverly Hills: Sage, 1977.

21. Jan Servaes. *One World, Multiple Cultures: A New Paradigm on Communication for Development*. Leuven, Belgium: ACCO, 1989.

22. Gerald Sussman and John A. Lent, ed. *Transnational Communication: Wiring the Third World*. Newbury Park: Sage, 1990.

23. Majid Tehranian. *Technologies of Power: Information Machines and Democratic Prospects*. New Jersey: Ablex, 1990.

INDEX

ABOUT THE AUTHOR

Bella Mody is Associate Professor of Telecommunication and Assistant Dean of Urban Studies at Michigan State University. Prior to this, she was on the Communication faculty at San Francisco State University (1984-1985) and at Stanford University (1978-1983). She has held visiting positions at Santa Clara University and at the Annenberg School at the University of Southern California.

Bella Mody has also been a Social Scientist on the Indian Space Research Organization's Satellite Instructional Television Experiment team (1972-1976); Manager of its Formative Research and Utilization Cell (1976-1977); and an advertising writer in J. Walter Thompson, Calcutta (1968-1969). She has had field experience with communication projects in Nepal, Thailand, Ghana, Tanzania, Zimbabwe, Kenya, Liberia, Jamaica, Barbados, and Costa Rica through consulting assignments with the World Health Organization, the World Bank, UNESCO, USAID, Dutch Aid, and Worldview International Foundation. Dr. Mody's recent research includes contextual analysis of communication technology in Third World countries. She has contributed several articles to reputed journals and edited volumes.